Historical American Biographies

DOUGLAS MACARTHUR

Brilliant General, Controversial Leader

Ann Graham Gaines

Enslow Publishers, Inc.

40 Industrial Road   PO Box 38
Box 398   Aldershot
Berkeley Heights, NJ 07922 Hants GU12 6BP
USA   UK

http://www.enslow.com

Library of Congress Cataloging-in-Publication Data

Gaines, Ann Graham.
    Douglas MacArthur : brilliant general, controversial leader /Ann
Graham Gaines.
        p. cm. — (Historical American biographies)
    Includes bibliographical references and index.
    ISBN 0-7660-1445-2
    1. MacArthur, Douglas, 1880–1964—Juvenile literature. 2. Generals—
United States—Biography—Juvenile literature. 3. United States. Army—
Biography—Juvenile literature. 4. United States—History, Military—
20th century—Juvenile literature.   [1. MacArthur, Douglas,
1880–1964. 2. Generals.]   I. Title. II. Series.
E745.M3.G27 2001
355'.0092—dc21
                                        00-009710

Printed in the United States of America

10 9 8 7 6 5 4 3 2 1

To Our Readers: All Internet Addresses in this book were active and appropriate
at the time we went to press. Any comments or suggestions can be sent by e-mail
to Comments@enslow.com or to the address on the back cover.

Illustration Credits: Enslow Publishers, pp. 24, 33, 74, 98; Library of
Congress, pp. 80, 101; National Archives, pp. 4, 55; Reproduced from
the *Dictionary of American Portraits*, Published by Dover Publications,
Inc., in 1967, p. 107; United States Army, pp. 7, 12, 21, 37, 41, 43, 51,
59, 61, 63, 82, 84, 94, 102, 110, 116.

Cover Illustrations: National Archives (Inset); © Corel Corporation
(Background).

CONTENTS

Douglas MacArthur

1

"I SHALL RETURN"

In 1942, United States General Douglas MacArthur was forced to flee the Philippines, a group of islands in the western Pacific Ocean. The Japanese, whom he had been fighting for months, threatened to overrun his forces. He left his headquarters on Corregidor Island with his family and a few aides in boats and headed south toward the safety of Australia. Thousands of American soldiers remained behind on the peninsula of Bataan. Those left behind would soon be killed or captured by the Japanese.

When MacArthur got to Australia, he wanted to reassure the people of the Philippines that he had not abandoned them for good. On March 20, 1942, he made a statement to reporters: "The President of the

United States ordered me to break through the Japanese lines . . . for the purpose, as I understand it, of organizing the American offensive against Japan, a primary object of which is the relief of the Philippines. I came through and I shall return."[1]

These would become some of the most famous words spoken during World War II, being fought by the United States and its allies against Japan, Germany, and Italy. Critics pointed out that General MacArthur really should have said, "We shall return," acknowledging that he would be accompanied by American troops when he returned to the Philippines. But Filipino journalist Carlos Romulo had pointed out that the words *We shall return* would not reassure Filipinos. The Filipinos had lost faith in the United States' ability and desire to protect them. But the Filipinos loved Douglas MacArthur as an individual. They would believe a promise MacArthur made.

Douglas MacArthur later wrote that his words did reassure the Filipinos. A very proud man, he said:

> "I shall return" seemed a promise of magic to the Filipinos. It lit a flame that became a symbol which focused the nation's indomitable will. . . . It was scraped in the sands of the beaches, it was daubed on the walls of the *barrios*, it was stamped on the mail, it was whispered in the cloisters of the church. It became the battle cry of a great underground swell that no Japanese bayonet could still.[2]

MacArthur biographer William Manchester doubted that the words had quite that much impact. But historians do acknowledge that the phrase, used over and over again, helped keep spirits high.

By 1944, the United States and the Allies had begun a massive drive through the Pacific Ocean. MacArthur had fought his way back from Australia. As MacArthur's army troops neared Japan, United States President Franklin Delano Roosevelt and the navy planned to have them bypass the Philippines, to wait until later to free the islands from Japanese rule. But MacArthur convinced American officials that the Philippines were "strategically vital" and that the Americans owed it to the Filipinos to rescue them from Japanese rule as soon as possible.[3]

General Douglas MacArthur is seen here (wearing sunglasses at center), wading ashore at Luzon in the Philippines.

So a new Philippines campaign was launched in September 1944. Seven hundred ships, hundreds of planes, and one hundred sixty thousand men gathered to invade Leyte Island, the southernmost of the many islands that make up the Philippines. On October 20, 1944, the assault began. After he waded ashore, MacArthur made a triumphal speech celebrating the fulfillment of his promise. He began, "People of the Philippines: I have returned. . . ."[4]

┌─────┐
│ 2 │
└─────┘

CHILDHOOD

Douglas MacArthur was born to Arthur and Mary Hardy MacArthur on January 26, 1880, in an army barracks in Little Rock, Arkansas.[1] MacArthur was very proud of his ancestry, which was Scottish on his father's side. As an old man, he quoted a proverb that said, "There is nothing older, except the hills, MacArtair [the Gaelic spelling of MacArthur] and the devil."[2] According to legend, members of the MacArthur family had been "linked with the heroic lore of King Arthur and the Knights of the Round Table."[3] MacArthurs had also fought in the Crusades, the wars in which European knights fought to drive Muslims out of Jerusalem.

In 1825, Sarah MacArthur, a widow, brought her ten-year-old son, Arthur, to the United States from

Scotland. Arthur MacArthur grew up to be an attorney. In 1855, he was elected lieutenant governor of the state of Wisconsin. After the governor resigned his office over charges of vote tampering, Arthur MacArthur stepped in, but for only five days. A court ruled that the governor's opponent had actually won the election, and that man then took over. In 1870, MacArthur was appointed by President Ulysses S. Grant to the judicial court that heard cases concerning crimes committed in the District of Columbia.[4]

Douglas MacArthur's Father

In 1845, Arthur MacArthur had a son, also named Arthur. He would later become General Douglas MacArthur's father. When the Civil War broke out in 1861, the younger Arthur MacArthur begged his father to allow him to join the Union Army even though he was only fifteen years old.[5] Instead, his father sent him to a private military academy. Arthur's teachers were impressed with his ability to understand military tactics and strategy. They recommended that he enroll in the United States Military Academy at West Point. However, there were no vacancies at West Point at the time.

Back at home, on August 4, 1862, Arthur MacArthur, Jr., signed up as a first lieutenant with the 24th Wisconsin Volunteer Infantry. He went off to fight on the side of the Union in the Civil War. He fought so fiercely in his first battle, at Perryville, Kentucky, on October 8, 1862, that he was promoted to captain and commended for bravery. At the battle of Stone's River near Murfreesboro, Tennessee, he unexpectedly had to assume command of his regiment when every other mounted officer was killed or injured. Union General Philip Sheridan gave him special commendation after both of these battles.

In another battle, Arthur MacArthur was shot, but a wallet containing a tiny Bible in his chest pocket stopped the bullet from entering his heart. After the Battle of Missionary Ridge, Tennessee, fought in November 1863, he was given command of his unit. In a bloody battle at Franklin, also in Tennessee, he was shot twice, once in the leg and once in the chest. His wounds kept him out of future battles. He spent the rest of the Civil War allowing his wounds to heal. In March 1865, the army recognized his service and promoted him to brevet colonel. He became the youngest colonel in the Union Army.[6] Two months later, he was promoted to lieutenant colonel.[7] In 1870, he received the Congressional Medal of Honor, the highest award an American soldier can receive, for his heroics at Missionary Ridge.

When the war ended with a Union victory in 1865, Arthur MacArthur left the army. He started to study law, intending to become an attorney like his father. But he found this life too boring. In February 1866, he joined the military again.

Arthur MacArthur served first as a second lieutenant in the 17th Regular Infantry. Promoted to first lieutenant, he transferred to the 36th Infantry, where he advanced to the rank of captain. In the years following

Douglas MacArthur's father, Arthur, won the Congressional Medal of Honor for his heroism in the Civil War.

Indian Wars

By the time of the Civil War, whites had begun to settle across much of the West. The American Indians had been living a nomadic (wandering) life, moving from camp to camp throughout the year. The federal government wanted American Indians to settle down. To achieve this, it had started to establish reservations. Some tribes gave up their lands and settled peacefully, if reluctantly, on reservations. Others, however, fought fiercely to be allowed to maintain their traditional way of life. The United States Army fought battle after battle with these Indians from the 1860s through the 1880s.

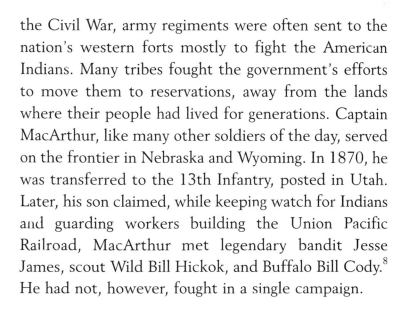

the Civil War, army regiments were often sent to the nation's western forts mostly to fight the American Indians. Many tribes fought the government's efforts to move them to reservations, away from the lands where their people had lived for generations. Captain MacArthur, like many other soldiers of the day, served on the frontier in Nebraska and Wyoming. In 1870, he was transferred to the 13th Infantry, posted in Utah. Later, his son claimed, while keeping watch for Indians and guarding workers building the Union Pacific Railroad, MacArthur met legendary bandit Jesse James, scout Wild Bill Hickok, and Buffalo Bill Cody.[8] He had not, however, fought in a single campaign.

The MacArthur Family

In 1874, Arthur MacArthur's company was transferred to New Orleans, Louisiana. Louisiana was then under military occupation, as were many former Confederate states, as part of Reconstruction. The North put troops in the South to keep order as the states rejoined the Union and adjusted to life without slavery. Having been a hero in Civil War battles, MacArthur now saw no action and no further opportunities to win glory. He did, however, find happiness in his personal life.

That winter during Mardi Gras, he met Mary Pinkney Hardy, known to her friends as Pinky. She was visiting New Orleans from Norfolk, Virginia. The two began a courtship that they maintained through letters even after she returned home.

In May 1875, MacArthur, on a three-month leave, went to Virginia to marry Pinky, a member of an old, aristocratic Virginia family that had arrived in the American colonies and helped found the Jamestown colony in 1607. Hardy's ancestors had fought in the American Revolution. Her brothers had fought for the Confederacy in the Civil War. Some of them considered her marriage to Arthur, a former Union soldier, an outrage. They refused to come to the wedding.

After they married, they moved to Washington, D.C., where Arthur worked in the army's offices. In 1876, he was assigned once more to New Orleans. There, he became commander of Company K of the 13th Infantry. His company moved frequently over the next four years, from post to post in Louisiana and Arkansas. In the meantime, the family expanded. Together, Arthur and Pinky MacArthur had three children: Arthur, born in 1876; Malcolm, born in 1878; and Douglas, born in 1880, in Little Rock, Arkansas.[9]

Five months after the birth of Douglas MacArthur, Company K was transferred to Fort Wingate, New Mexico. While the family lived there, tragedy struck. Their second son, Malcolm, died of measles at the age of five.[10] The entire family mourned him. Pinky MacArthur transported his body all the way back to Virginia to bury Malcolm in her family's cemetery plot.

In 1884, Arthur's Company K—which included just two officers, forty-six enlisted men, and a doctor—was ordered to march three hundred miles to Fort Selden, about sixty miles north of El Paso, Texas. Their mission was to prevent Apache Chief Geronimo from attacking travelers as they crossed the Rio Grande. The MacArthur family went along.

Douglas MacArthur later said his earliest memories were of that march. As a child, he grew to love "the sound of Army bugles."[11] Years later, Douglas MacArthur still remembered how exciting life had been on the frontier. He reminisced about watching the soldiers' nightly ceremony of retreat, at which the American flag was lowered as the sun went down.

During their years at Fort Selden, Arthur and Douglas were taught to read and write by their mother. But what they really enjoyed was the other education they received: "I learned to ride and shoot even before

I could read or write—indeed, almost before I could walk and talk," Douglas MacArthur claimed.[12] The family would always remain close. There were few other children at Fort Selden, but the boys had each other to play soldiers and Indians with.

In 1886, after Chief Geronimo finally surrendered, Company K was ordered to Fort Leavenworth, Kansas, where the army had just established a training school. Fort Leavenworth was a much larger army post than Douglas had ever seen. Douglas remained fascinated with the sights and sounds of the army. He went out of his way to watch the cavalry ride and the infantrymen drill, with their bayonets glittering at the end of their rifles.

In Kansas, Douglas enrolled in public school for the first time, entering second grade. He was very unhappy in school, especially at the beginning. He missed the time he and his mother had spent working together on his lessons. He also missed the freedom he had enjoyed on the frontier.[13]

Arthur MacArthur Rises in the Army

In 1889, the family moved again after Arthur MacArthur received a promotion to major. Now the family lived in a big, bustling city. But they still socialized mostly with the children of other officers, playing games that revolved around guns and war.

Their father's next transfer came in 1893. By this time, Arthur MacArthur III was enrolled at the United States Naval Academy in Annapolis, Maryland.

The senior Arthur, Pinky, and Douglas went to Fort Sam Houston, in San Antonio, Texas. At age thirteen, Douglas was in the eighth grade. At "Fort Sam," the MacArthurs lived in luxurious officers' quarters. They even had a maid.[14]

In 1893, Douglas enrolled at the West Texas Military Academy in San Antonio. He did very well there, both in his studies and in sports. He won the school's trophy for tennis. He played quarterback for the football team and shortstop for the baseball team. In the school military company to which he belonged, he received a promotion to first major. He also organized a drill unit that soon received invitations to exhibit its skills at other schools.

Fort Sam Houston

Fort Selden, like other western posts to which Arthur MacArthur was assigned, was tiny and isolated. When the MacArthur family lived there, they roughed it. Living in plain adobe buildings, they cooked and bathed with water hauled from the river.

Fort Sam Houston, however, was a large, new complex located on the outskirts of the city of San Antonio, Texas. Construction of Fort Sam, as the locals called it, began in 1876. By the time the MacArthurs arrived there, it boasted a large quadrangle, or green space, surrounded by buildings, a hospital, and handsome two-story homes for officers.[15]

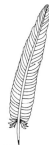

Preparing for West Point

Douglas MacArthur graduated from the academy in 1897 with a gold medal for outstanding scholarship. By then, his father had been transferred to St. Paul, Minnesota. Douglas and his mother, however, had stayed behind so Douglas could finish school.

After his graduation, Douglas and his mother moved to Milwaukee, Wisconsin. Douglas's mother hoped that a congressman from Milwaukee—Theabold Otjen, who had been a friend of Douglas's grandfather—would appoint him to the United States Military Academy at West Point. There was also a doctor in Milwaukee whom Mrs. MacArthur wanted to consult about Douglas's curvature of the spine. Unless this condition could be corrected, he could not pass the West Point physical.[16]

To prepare for West Point, MacArthur had to study with a tutor for an entire year. On June 7, 1898, the local newspaper ran an article announcing that Douglas MacArthur had placed first among all of the applicants who had taken the West Point exam in Milwaukee.[17] For another year, he had to do the exercises the doctor had prescribed to help him overcome his spinal curvature. Then off to West Point he went.

3

ARMY

Having decided to follow in his father's footsteps and pursue a career in the army, Douglas MacArthur attended the military academy at West Point from 1899 to 1903. Enrolling there meant another move, but it did not remove him from his family. MacArthur's mother moved to New York with him. While Douglas lived in a dormitory at West Point, Mrs. MacArthur was never more than a few blocks away. She lived in a nearby hotel while he went to school.[1]

West Point
When he first arrived at West Point, Douglas MacArthur had to endure hazing—the punishment older students traditionally give new arrivals. His fellow students

teased him about his father, who was becoming famous, and about his close relationship with his mother. During his second year, MacArthur was called as a witness to testify before Congress concerning hazing at West Point. He appeared, but refused to name any upperclassmen who still attended the school. All those he named had either confessed already, or had left West Point.[2]

During his four years at the academy, MacArthur studied hard. Like all students at West Point, he took classes in mathematics, history, law, military engineering, geography, chemistry, geology, English, Spanish, and French. Students also had to train for life as an army officer. Day after day they drilled, practicing precise turns and about-faces. At gunnery practice, they shot cannons. MacArthur liked everything about it. Later, he described his experience at West Point as a "thrill."[3]

In 1903, MacArthur graduated from West Point first in his class. While there, he had earned the military rank of first captain (the highest rank a student could achieve). He had also earned a grade point average of 98.14, the highest of any student in twenty-five years.[4] His class voted him most likely to succeed.

To the Philippines

After graduation, Douglas MacArthur's career as an army officer began. He was commissioned a second lieutenant in the Army Corps of Engineers. In June 1903, he was sent to his first military posting in the Philippines.

Douglas MacArthur studied hard to have one of highest grade point averages in West Point's history. He graduated first in his class.

The Philippines is a country made up of many small islands, located off China and Vietnam in the Pacific Ocean. In 1521, Ferdinand Magellan and his crew became the first Europeans to see these islands when they sailed around the world. Spain claimed them as a colony and began to send settlers there in 1565. The islands were still a Spanish colony in 1898, when the Spanish-American War broke out. The United States declared war on Spain after an American battleship, the *Maine*, exploded in a harbor in Spanish-owned Cuba. When the *Maine* blew up, Americans believed the Spanish had mined it. Congress voted to use the military to try to force Spain to grant Cuba its independence. But the war would not be limited to Cuba. The United States Navy's Pacific fleet also attacked Spanish ships in the Philippines.

On May 1, 1898, American ships captured or destroyed all the Spanish ships anchored in Manila Bay. On July 17, Spain asked for a truce. Fighting stopped and peace negotiations opened. Although Americans generally believed that Spain no longer had a right to the Philippines, the United States did not think it should be granted independence. The two nations signed a treaty of peace in December. In it, Spain recognized Cuba's independence and agreed to give the United States the Philippines, Puerto Rico, and Guam in exchange for $20 million. In the meantime, rebel forces had begun a guerrilla war in the Philippines to win the nation's independence.

Douglas MacArthur's father, Arthur, had gone to the Philippines during the Spanish-American War. He commanded the troops that occupied Manila in August 1898.[5] As military governor of the Philippines, it was Arthur MacArthur who crushed the revolt led by Emilio Aguinaldo, a Filipino nationalist.[6] Under his orders, American soldiers captured Aguinaldo and brought him to Manila, where he swore an oath of allegiance to the United States. The capture and capitulation of their leader did not, however, crush the guerrillas' spirits. The Filipino resistance movement would continue for another ten years.[7]

By the time Douglas MacArthur arrived in the Philippines, Arthur MacArthur was back in the United States. General Adna R. Chafee took over command of the American troops stationed there.[8] As an army engineer, Douglas MacArthur helped survey Filipino roads and harbors. He also experienced some danger. Once, while he was in the jungle working on a road, he was attacked by two guerrilla fighters. One of them shot a bullet right through his hat. MacArthur quickly pulled out his pistol and killed both men.[9]

The Russo-Japanese War and Asia

Douglas MacArthur was transferred to San Francisco in October 1904. He had developed a fierce love for the Philippines and was sorry to leave it.

In California, he studied engineering and received a promotion to first lieutenant. On October 3, 1905, he got a new appointment as aide-de-camp—secretary and assistant—to his father, by then a major general

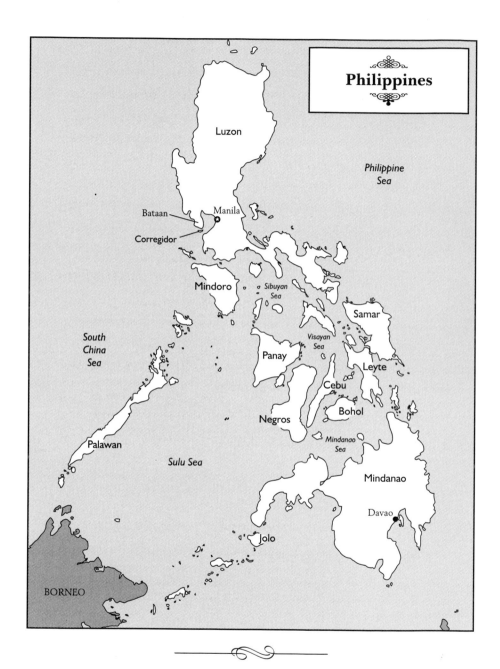

Douglas MacArthur fell in love with the Philippine Islands the first time he was stationed there. They would play a vital role in his later career.

who was being sent back to Asia. War had broken out in 1904 between Russia and Japan, both of which hoped to acquire new territory in Asia. The Russian Army had occupied the Chinese province of Manchuria. The Japanese, who wanted both Manchuria and Korea, attacked Russian Navy ships anchored in a Manchurian port.

United States President Theodore Roosevelt did not want to see any one empire have too much power in the Far East. He wanted very much for the war to end before this happened. He intended to invite delegates from both nations to a peace conference. Before he could do this, he needed accurate information about what was going on in Asia. So he sent Americans to tour the area. Accompanied by Pinky, Arthur and Douglas MacArthur visited military bases in Japan and then traveled to China, Hong Kong, Java, Singapore, Burma, and India, gathering information for President Roosevelt.

Engineering School

The army sent Douglas MacArthur back to engineering school in Washington, D.C., in 1906. He proved to be a poor student. He now preferred traveling to sitting in a classroom. On December 4, he got a second assignment. He became an aide-de-camp to President Theodore Roosevelt. The president hoped to gain further knowledge of Asia from MacArthur. MacArthur admired President Roosevelt because he was trying to increase the role of the United States in world affairs, asserting its might and protecting American business interests overseas.

Milwaukee

In 1907, MacArthur graduated from engineering school and made yet another transfer. This time he went to Milwaukee, where his parents then lived. There, he was assigned engineering duties. He did not perform them well. Historian William Manchester speculated that MacArthur's poor performance was due to demands made on him by his parents. His father, who retired from the army in 1909, was bored.[10] Pinky MacArthur wanted her son to take her shopping and to parties.

Eventually, MacArthur's commanding officer, Major William V. Judson, ordered him to supervise the reconstruction of a harbor sixty miles north of Milwaukee. MacArthur argued that he did not want to leave his parents. Judson insisted, and MacArthur went north until the winter arrived, making it impossible to work on the harbor. In the spring, MacArthur

Corps of Engineers

The United States Army has included a Corps of Engineers for more than two hundred fifty years. The engineers not only design and construct army and air force bases and buildings, but they also plan and build projects that make rivers and harbors navigable.[11]

went back to work on the harbor. Five days later, he got orders relieving him of his present duty and sending him instead to Fort Leavenworth.

At the end of the year, Major Judson had to write efficiency reports about everyone who had been under his command at any time during the previous year— including MacArthur. Judson criticized MacArthur in the report. On seeing it, MacArthur went over Judson's head and complained to Brigadier General William Marshall, chief of the army engineers. Marshall scolded MacArthur for ignoring the chain of command. He said, "The Chief of Engineers expects of all officers under his command promptness and alacrity in obeying orders, and faithful performance of duties assigned them."[12] MacArthur realized that he had to change his ways and begin to cooperate if he hoped to be promoted to senior officer someday. In the meantime, Pinky tried to find MacArthur a civilian job. But MacArthur was soon enjoying life in the army once again, having been assigned command of Company K. According to MacArthur, when he took over command of the company it was always the "lowest-rated" at inspection time.[13] He worked hard to build his men's morale and skills. Soon they did better than anyone else at general inspection.

On the Engineer Board

MacArthur was promoted to captain on February 11, 1911. Leaving Fort Leavenworth, he was assigned to the army's Engineer Board. In this capacity, he was sent on a series of tours of duty. During one of these tours, he went to Panama. There, the United States was building the Panama Canal to connect the Gulf of Mexico and the Pacific Ocean. Once the work was completed, the army would need defenses there. MacArthur helped plan them.[14]

Arthur MacArthur died on September 5, 1912, while attending his Civil War regiment's fiftieth reunion. He collapsed midway through a speech, a victim of apoplexy (his neurological functions had suddenly stopped). Once he was pronounced dead, his former aide covered his body with the regimental flag. The aide then fell to the floor. He, too, had suffered a stroke that would prove fatal.[15]

After her husband's death, Pinky MacArthur fell ill. Douglas MacArthur asked the army for a transfer to Milwaukee but was refused. Instead, he moved his mother to Leavenworth.

Washington, D.C.

Soon the Army Chief of Staff, Major General Leonard Wood, ordered MacArthur to Washington, D.C. His mother moved there to be with her son. He was appointed to the army's general staff.

In this new position, MacArthur did office work—compiling statistics and writing reports. But he also got to know and observe the highest-ranking officials in the American army.

During this period, he also got a taste of combat. In April 1914, the United States and Mexico were on the brink of war. A general named Victoriano Huerta had seized control of Mexico. The United States refused to recognize Huerta's new government. On April 22, the secretary of war asked Major General Wood to get the army ready to fight in Mexico. Lacking reliable information about what was going on south of the border, Wood ordered MacArthur to act as a spy for him.

On May 1, 1914, MacArthur left the U.S.S. *Nebraska* in Veracruz, on the east coast of Mexico. The United States Navy had already seized the city and an army brigade occupied it. Eleven thousand Mexican soldiers, however, had begun a siege. They had surrounded the city and were trying to capture it.

MacArthur was supposed to report to the local American commander. Unable to find him, however, MacArthur disobeyed his orders and headed out by himself into the Mexican countryside. He wanted to find out whether he could use railroads to enter the

Mexico in 1914

In 1914, Mexico was in an uproar. Three years earlier, Francisco Madero had led a revolt that overthrew the government of President Porfirio Diaz. In 1913, Madero himself had been killed by Mexican soldiers loyal to General Victoriano Huerta. The American government refused to recognize the Huerta government and sent seven thousand troops to occupy the port of Veracruz. After five hundred Mexicans died in fighting with Americans, Huerta resigned and the American forces withdrew.

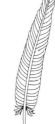

city if Wood had to bring more troops in. MacArthur persuaded three railroad men to lead him out of the city. They traveled by handcar (a small open railroad car that used a pump to move), canoe, and on foot until MacArthur found five locomotives that the Americans could use. On the way back, five armed men attacked MacArthur and his companions. Later, he faced three more. Before he recrossed American lines, MacArthur had to kill six men.[16]

From Veracruz, MacArthur returned to the United States to make his report to Wood. Wood, however, never used the information MacArthur had gathered. The threat of war passed when Huerta resigned. Nevertheless, Wood recommended MacArthur for a Congressional Medal of Honor for his efforts. The board of awards, however, rejected the recommendation. The board feared giving the medal to MacArthur might encourage other officers to ignore local commands and strike out on their own. MacArthur, unwisely, registered an official protest. He called the board rigid, narrow-minded, and unimaginative. This only helped to cement some army officials' view of him as a temperamental man who wanted special attention and favors. Such opinions would hurt him later in his career.

4

WAR!

World War I broke out in Europe on July 28, 1914, when the European nation of Austria declared war on Serbia, its eastern neighbor. A month earlier, an assassin with ties to nationalists in Serbia—people fighting for Serbian independence—had killed Austrian Archduke Franz Ferdinand. Alliances brought many other European countries into the war. Russia entered on the side of Serbia. Germany declared war on Russia and France, which was allied with Russia. Great Britain entered the war on the side of Russia and France. Eventually, Italy also joined the Allies, which included Russia, France, and Great Britain.

The United States did not immediately join the Allies. American President Woodrow Wilson initially issued a statement declaring the United States neutral. Most Americans supported him. They did not want to send American soldiers across the ocean to fight in a war they saw as far removed from them. Public sentiment would change, however, after Germany sank the British passenger ship *Lusitania*, killing more than one thousand people, including 128 Americans. The United States would finally enter World War I in April 1917.

Getting Ready for War

Upon his return from Mexico in 1914, Douglas MacArthur had returned to the army's general staff. It was a time of tremendous activity in its offices in Washington. The army had to get ready in case the United States decided to enter the war in Europe.

In December 1915, the army promoted MacArthur to major. In 1916, Secretary of War Newton Baker appointed MacArthur as his assistant. MacArthur's duties included handling public relations for the army. Through press releases and interviews with journalists, he helped persuade people to support the selective service act Congress passed on May 18, 1917. This law meant that there was a draft—the military could select people to serve rather than wait for volunteers to join.

MacArthur also played an important role in persuading the president to send National Guard troops to fight in Europe. The National Guard had been formed in 1916. At first, army officials did not want to use the Guard. Instead, they proposed to draft an

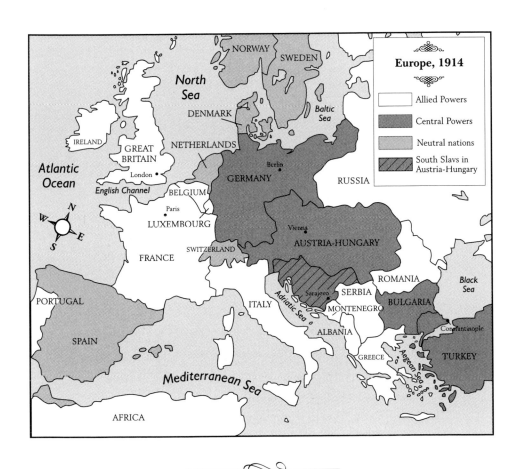

Europe, 1914

- Allied Powers
- Central Powers
- Neutral nations
- South Slavs in Austria-Hungary

NORWAY

SWEDEN

North Sea

DENMARK

Baltic Sea

IRELAND

GREAT BRITAIN

NETHERLANDS

Berlin

GERMANY

RUSSIA

Atlantic Ocean

English Channel

London

BELGIUM

Paris

LUXEMBOURG

Vienna

AUSTRIA-HUNGARY

FRANCE

SWITZERLAND

ROMANIA

Black Sea

PORTUGAL

ITALY

Adriatic Sea

Sarajevo

SERBIA

MONTENEGRO

BULGARIA

Constantinople

SPAIN

ALBANIA

Aegean Sea

GREECE

TURKEY

Mediterranean Sea

AFRICA

World War I eventually came to include most of the powers of Europe, as well as the United States.

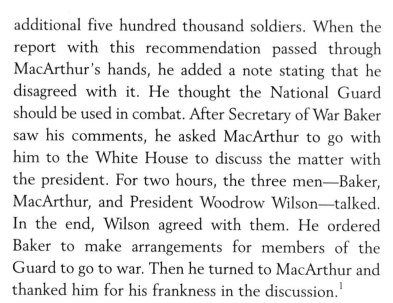

National Guard

Today, every state still has its own National Guard units—military reserves who stand ready in case the army suddenly needs extra people. Those who join the National Guard work regular jobs but report for training and duty some weekends and for two weeks each summer.

The federal government could one day use the National Guard again in war. Both the federal and state governments can also call on the Guard in times of emergency, such as natural disasters.

additional five hundred thousand soldiers. When the report with this recommendation passed through MacArthur's hands, he added a note stating that he disagreed with it. He thought the National Guard should be used in combat. After Secretary of War Baker saw his comments, he asked MacArthur to go with him to the White House to discuss the matter with the president. For two hours, the three men—Baker, MacArthur, and President Woodrow Wilson—talked. In the end, Wilson agreed with them. He ordered Baker to make arrangements for members of the Guard to go to war. Then he turned to MacArthur and thanked him for his frankness in the discussion.[1]

One problem then remained. The National Guard's troops were organized by state. Which state's men should be sent to war first? Members of the public might protest if their state Guard were selected to go first. When Baker brought up this question in a meeting with MacArthur and Brigadier General William A. Mann, Mann suggested that a division might be formed including National Guard members from several states. MacArthur said, "Fine, that will stretch over the whole country like a rainbow."[2] Thus was formed the 42nd National Guard Division, which would be nicknamed the Rainbow Division.

Mann was appointed commander of the Rainbow Division. MacArthur would be Mann's chief of staff. When MacArthur pointed out that he was ineligible for this position because he was only a major, he was immediately promoted to colonel. He also transferred from the Army Engineer Corps to the infantry. Biographers often say MacArthur made this change because he knew more promotions went to that division than to the Corps of Engineers. MacArthur later said he simply wanted to fight in the same division his father had.[3]

The Rainbow Division Goes to Europe

Mann and MacArthur spent two months assembling the 42nd Division in Long Island, New York. The division included twenty-seven thousand soldiers. On October 18, 1917, the Rainbow Division, including Douglas MacArthur, boarded ships in New Jersey and sailed for Europe.

The voyage across the Atlantic Ocean was hard. The ships were crowded. Everyone had to wear lifebelts (lifejackets) around the clock because of the possibility that they would be attacked by enemy submarines. At night, the ships were kept completely dark so they could not be spotted from afar. The men practiced military drills every day.

Thirteen days after they set sail, the ships neared France. However, the *Covington*, the ship MacArthur was on, ran aground near the mouth of the Loire River. When an enemy submarine was spotted, several patrol boats arrived to protect the *Covington*. The ship was finally freed, but by that point, there was no place for it to anchor in the harbor. MacArthur and his fellow passengers had to spend another three days aboard.

Finally, they arrived at St. Nazaire. Their first month in France was spent training in the Meuse Valley. General John J. Pershing, leader of the American Expeditionary Force in France, almost immediately ordered thirty-three of the Rainbow Division's best officers to other units. Army officials also wanted to use men from the 42nd to replace those killed in other divisions.

MacArthur protested by sending a series of telegrams to Washington, D.C. He was never one to avoid stating his opinion or complaining. Eventually, Pershing was persuaded to leave the Rainbow Division intact. However, MacArthur's actions made a group of high-ranking officers dislike him. In turn, MacArthur became suspicious that some people were out to get him.[4] Nevertheless, MacArthur remained tremendously popular with his men.

MacArthur annoyed some officers during World War I by protesting or ignoring orders.

On the Battlefield

The 42nd had to train for months in Lorraine, a province in northern France, to get ready for the terrible trench warfare of World War I. In February 1918, the 42nd marched into the Luneville sector in southern Lorraine, very near the battlefront. By this time, MacArthur was spending hour after hour on paperwork, drawing up plans for fighting and keeping his men supplied.

Conditions were harsh. It was constantly cold and wet, and he and his soldiers were hungry and tired. Yet MacArthur's spirits remained high. He believed in the cause for which he was fighting. And he was enjoying the test of his own strength. Throughout the war, he proved himself a capable officer, organized and able to build morale among his men.

On February 26, he got a chance to participate in a raid on German lines. A party of French soldiers was planning to race across the no-man's-land that divided German and Allied troops and stage a fast attack. MacArthur asked the French general in charge of the operation to let him go along. That night, the French soldiers and MacArthur climbed over their fortification's wall and started to cross the no-man's-land. They had to crawl over barbed wire and avoid falling into the huge holes left by exploded shells. As they reached the German line, one of the French soldiers threw a grenade to signal to his comrades it was time to attack. German machine guns fired round after round at them. But MacArthur and the others fought hard.

Trench Warfare
In World War I, soldiers who were engaged in combat on land spent many long hours in trenches. These trenches had been dug along the edges of the areas France held. Barbed wire ran along their tops. Troops who were ordered to hold a sector, or area, simply fought from inside the trenches. Troops who were ordered to advance into enemy territory had to leave the trenches and crawl or run toward the trenches of the enemy, while trying to evade enemy gunfire.

They finally managed to capture a large number of German soldiers, whom they then led back into French territory. The army awarded MacArthur the Silver Star, a medal for gallantry in action, for his part in the raid. The French Army also decorated him with the French Croix de Guerre, another medal of honor.

On March 9, MacArthur led an assault by hundreds of American soldiers into German trenches. He was one of the few high officers who actually accompanied his troops into battle. Two days later, he and his men were still in the trenches they had captured when Germans aimed shells filled with poison gas right at them. MacArthur rarely carried a gas mask, and he became sick, but soon recovered. His willingness to engage in close combat, fighting hand-to-hand and with bayonets and hand grenades, earned him a reputation as the "bloodiest fighting man in this army."[5]

In the following months, the Rainbow Division fought hard. By the time the war ended with an Allied victory on November 11, 1918, the division had suffered fourteen thousand casualties (dead, wounded, or missing soldiers). MacArthur bragged about his men's exploits. He liked to tell reporters that his men were on the front line, in the most heated part of battle, 180 of the 224 days they were on the front. He boasted of how many German soldiers his troops had taken prisoner. Army records also show that the Rainbow Division captured an extraordinary number of the enemy's artillery pieces and machine guns.[6]

MacArthur's Performance

MacArthur received praise for his record in World War I. He received a temporary promotion to the rank of major general. Some officers, however, complained that MacArthur refused to issue orders from the rear, always leading his own troops into battle. They thought he was taking too big a risk. But General Pershing told them, "Stop all this nonsense. MacArthur is the greatest leader of troops we have, and I intend to make him a division commander."[7] MacArthur received many decorations for his service, including seven Silver Stars, the Distinguished Service Medal, two Purple Hearts, and nineteen honors from Allied nations. Back in the United States, Americans read of his achievements in newspapers. They came to consider him a tremendously brave and dedicated soldier.

Here, General John J. Pershing awards MacArthur the Distinguished Service Medal for his service in World War I.

On November 22, MacArthur was relieved of his command of the Rainbow Division. On December 1, 1918, he entered Germany as the commander of the 84th Brigade. It would form one part of the American force that occupied Germany after the war. Allied soldiers were sent there to ensure that Germany did not try to rebuild its army and continue fighting. The 84th Brigade would stay in Germany for four months fulfilling this duty. Then, Douglas MacArthur would finally get to go home.

5

BACK HOME

Douglas MacArthur was stationed in Germany for four months after World War I ended. In March 1919, members of the Rainbow Division started to go home. Army commanders initially intended to leave MacArthur in Germany longer, but when news came that his mother was ill, he was ordered back to the United States. His brother Arthur, who served in the navy during World War I, also with great distinction, came home and assumed command of a naval training station in San Diego, California.[1]

Home
On April 25, 1919, Douglas MacArthur arrived in New York City. That night, a ball was held in his honor at the Waldorf Astoria hotel.[2] Thanks to reporters'

coverage of his exploits in the war in newspapers and radio reports, he had become one of the nation's most famous generals. The nation considered this smart, charming, hard-working, ambitious, political, courageous, and vain man a hero.

MacArthur's 84th Brigade was demobilized at Camp Dodge in May. Douglas MacArthur was then appointed superintendent of West Point, the military academy from which he had graduated almost twenty years earlier.

MacArthur (center) and the 84th Brigade occupied Germany after World War I to make sure the Germans would not rebuild their army.

Back to West Point

MacArthur became superintendent of West Point on June 12, 1919. Although most people in the United States, exhausted from World War I, could not bear the thought of any more fighting, MacArthur and other army officials realized that it was important for the country to remain ready for combat.

To make sure the service had enough well-trained officers, MacArthur made some important changes at the academy. During the war, students had been allowed to graduate after just one year of study. MacArthur changed this. West Point once again required four years of education before granting a degree. When he arrived at West Point, only two instructors there had graduated from a university. MacArthur hired more university graduates and paid for other West Point instructors to go and visit other colleges and universities to watch great professors teach.[3] Another one of MacArthur's goals was to see West Point's students become physically fit. Team sports became important. Visitors watched students perform complicated military maneuvers.

At the same time, MacArthur instituted strict rules against brutal hazing. At West Point, older students had a tradition of initiating new students by playing cruel practical jokes on them or forcing them to perform difficult and humiliating tasks. On January 1, 1919, a West Point student had committed suicide after being hazed without mercy. MacArthur wanted to make sure nothing like that ever happened again at

West Point. By the time he left, the size of the student body had almost doubled, which was especially notable because the army was decreasing in size due to the end of the war.[4]

Romance

When MacArthur first took over at West Point, he lived in the superintendent's mansion with his mother. This soon changed, however. MacArthur was a tall, slim man whom many women considered handsome. He had dated a lot as a young man but had never had a serious, long-term romance, probably because he was so determined to get ahead in the army.

After he returned from the war, however, he began to date Louise Cromwell Brookes. She was a wealthy divorced woman with two children. She lived outside Washington, D.C., and knew many army officers. In January 1922, they announced their engagement, and on February 14, 1922, they were married in Florida. MacArthur was then forty-two years old. MacArthur's mother disliked Louise so much that, when Louise moved into MacArthur's house at West Point, Pinky moved out. For the first time ever, Pinky and Douglas MacArthur were not on good terms.

Back to the Philippines

In the summer of 1922, Douglas MacArthur's tour of duty at West Point ended. He received a new overseas assignment—command of the Manila district in the Philippines. His new family—Louise and her children, Walter and Louise—went with him.

On October 22, 1922, the four of them landed in Manila. Although MacArthur enjoyed returning to the islands he would always love, the following years would be difficult for him on a personal level. His wife did not like life in the Philippines, which made their marriage rocky. He also missed his mother. Then, in 1923, his brother died unexpectedly of appendicitis.[5]

Within the army, rumors circulated that Army Chief of Staff General John J. Pershing was angry with MacArthur because of his marriage. Louise Brookes and Pershing were said to have been involved in a romance earlier. It was anger arising from jealousy, gossips concluded, that caused Pershing to give MacArthur the assignment of surveying the mountainous Bataan peninsula as part of drawing up plans for its defense.[6] Usually, such a duty would have been given to a junior

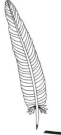

The Philippines
The nation of the Philippines is located in the western Pacific Ocean, east of Vietnam and south of Taiwan. Although the nation is made up of more than seven thousand islands, only eleven of these measure more than one thousand square miles.

Europeans first came to the Philippines in 1521. By the 1560s, Spain controlled the islands. In 1896, the Filipinos revolted against their Spanish government. After the Spanish-American War ended in 1898, Spain ceded the Philippines to the United States, which finally granted the nation full independence on July 4, 1946.

officer. Most of the time, MacArthur took offense
when he thought he was treated unfairly. But this time
he did not complain at all. He and his men did the survey. When they were done, on January 17, 1925,
Pershing rewarded MacArthur with a permanent promotion to major general.

III Corps

MacArthur's new rank made him overqualified for his
position in the Philippines. So, he returned to the
United States, where he became chief of III Corps.

The III Corps headquarters were located near
Baltimore, Maryland. The move especially pleased
Louise, who owned an estate in Baltimore County.
She had never grown used to living in the Philippines.
She came down with malaria, a tropical disease carried
by mosquitoes. Her son, Walter, was hurt there while
horseback riding. The climate was hot and sticky. Even
in the capital of Manila, there were far too few of the
fancy parties she loved.

Douglas MacArthur's new command was not very
exciting. He handled a lot of paperwork and watched
his men drill. Still, he put in a lot of extra time at his
job. Having learned that the number of pacifists (people opposed to war) in the United States was growing,
MacArthur worried that the nation was no longer
committed to military preparedness. He spent a lot of
time recruiting members for the army's high school
officer training program.

One of his most difficult duties during this period
came when he was ordered to serve as a judge at the

court-martial of Brigadier General William Mitchell. In the United States, members of the military follow special military laws. When accused of a crime, they are not tried in a regular courtroom but in a special military trial called a court-martial.

Mitchell had long been campaigning for the army to build up its air force. He thought airplanes could help the United States win future wars. In 1925, he told journalists that military officials were neglecting air power. The army charged him with violating the Articles of War by "conduct prejudicial to good order and military discipline."[7] In other words, his actions could have caused discipline to break down. His court-martial was highly publicized. At the end, the court found him guilty and suspended him from duty for five years. Although there is no record of how MacArthur—or any other individual member of the court—voted, MacArthur later wrote, "I did what I could in his behalf."[8]

The Olympics

In 1927, MacArthur got a special assignment, which temporarily released him from service in the army. He served as the head of the United States Olympic Committee. The committee chose him for the job because he had promoted sports both at West Point and as a corps commander, and because he was a popular public figure. He accompanied the nation's athletes to Amsterdam, Holland, where the games were held in 1928. There, he coached the American athletes. When the manager of the United States boxing team threatened to quit because a judge gave a decision that was unfair to an American boxer, MacArthur growled in the manager's face, "Americans never quit."[9] The American athletes set seventeen records. Their medals gave them a final score of 131 points, the highest of any country.

The Philippines Again

After the Olympics, MacArthur was named commander of the Philippine Department. This meant that he commanded all the military forces in the Philippines. His wife, Louise, had tired of army life. She encouraged him to resign from the army to become a business executive. He refused. She, in turn, refused to return to the Philippines. This proved to be the breaking point in their marriage. They divorced in 1929. MacArthur seems not to have minded. Years later, he would write that they suffered from "mutual incompatibility."[10]

MacArthur enjoyed his life in the Philippines. He had a lot to do. He liked the officers he worked with, and thought well of Manuel Quezon, the Filipino president. At the time, the Philippines still belonged to the United States, but both MacArthur and Quezon hoped the islands would soon be granted independence.[11]

At the time, Japan was growing in power. Observers considered it possible that one day it would wage war to win new territory. Quezon and MacArthur spent a great deal of time discussing Japan's intentions. Recently, many Japanese had immigrated to the Philippine island of Mindanao. Some suspected that they might one day try to take over the island. It also seemed possible that Japan might invade China. MacArthur, Quezon, and other Filipinos wanted to make sure that, should Japan show interest in taking over the Philippines as well, the islands would be able to defend themselves.[12] The American army was prepared to help them acquire arms and military skills.

Army Chief of Staff

In 1929, President Herbert Hoover approached MacArthur about a new assignment as chief of the Army Engineers. MacArthur said he was not interested. He believed he lacked the engineering expertise the position required.

His refusal let him accept another assignment instead. On August 6, 1930, President Hoover announced

Army Chief of Staff

The United States Army's senior officer was called the Commanding General from 1775 until 1903. Since then, he or she has been called the Army Chief of Staff.[13]

The Chief of Staff is responsible for all army operations. All Chiefs of Staff rise through army ranks. Chiefs of army divisions such as the Corps of Engineers report to them. Along with the Chiefs of the Navy and the Air Force, the Army Chief of Staff is a member of the Joint Chiefs of Staff.

he had plans to appoint MacArthur the Army Chief of Staff, which meant he would be the official in charge of the army. He would oversee the "command, discipline, training, and recruitment of the Army, military operations, distribution of troops, inspections, armament, fortifications. . . ."[14] MacArthur left the Philippines in September. On November 21, he was sworn in as Chief of Staff. At the same time, he received a promotion to the rank of four-star general. Then fifty, he was the youngest man to assume the Army Chief of Staff position to date.

His new job brought MacArthur back to Washington, D.C. He and his mother lived together once again, this time in a mansion on the Potomac River. In his position, MacArthur's biggest challenge was using a limited budget to re-equip the army, which had modernized very little since the end of World War I. The Great Depression, a long period during which the American economy

MacArthur was Army Chief of Staff under Presidents Hoover and Franklin Roosevelt.

The Great Depression

The United States enjoyed a period of great prosperity throughout almost all of the 1920s. In October 1929, however, the American stock market crashed, setting off the beginning of the Great Depression, a period of severe recession. The crash was caused partly by wild speculation in stocks on the part of investors. Although President Herbert Hoover initially predicted that the economy would recover quickly, the country suffered terribly for years. By 1933, more than fifty-five hundred banks had closed. Factories shut down. Thousands of farmers lost their land. Unemployment had soared to 25 percent in 1933. President Franklin Delano Roosevelt's New Deal programs offered federal relief and instituted reforms that put people back to work. Jobs remained too few, however. In 1939, 17 percent of the labor force was still out of work.

crumbled, was then under way. The nation gave fewer funds to the army every year.

As part of his job, MacArthur toured army bases, including those in Europe. He made one trip to Europe in 1931 and another a year later. There, his importance was recognized. Many heads of state met with him to discuss their own countries' military situations.

The Bonus Army

His years as Chief of Staff were happy times for MacArthur. He was very proud of his accomplishments, including his rapid rise through the army's ranks. However, he also had one difficult experience while he held the position.

In 1932, the Great Depression was continuing to cause suffering all across the country. Millions of people were out of work. Many families had lost their homes. Many men had left their families to go on the road to look for work.

Years earlier, veterans of World War I had been offered a bonus for their service. The government had originally planned to pay the bonus in 1945. But when the Depression began to hurt so many, some veterans began to demand that the bonus be paid early. In the summer of 1932, more than fifteen thousand protesters—veterans and their families—arrived in Washington, D.C., hoping to convince Congress to pay the bonus. At night, the protesters camped right in the middle of the nation's capital. They became known as the Bonus Army. Despite their efforts, the Senate refused to pay the bonus. Seeking to convince them to give up their protests, President Herbert Hoover signed a bill providing them loans to use for transportation home. Many took the money and left Washington, D.C. But others stayed.

The situation became worse. On July 28, 1932, a scuffle broke out between protesters and police on the steps of the Capitol. President Hoover asked

MacArthur to handle the problem. MacArthur took six hundred soldiers and marched on the protesters' camp.

Hoover had told him directly to make sure that no one was hurt. But MacArthur ordered the veterans' makeshift shelters set on fire. He also had his men gas the camp. By the end of the day, two veterans had died.

Later, it became clear that, although MacArthur had believed that most of the protesters were dangerous, almost all the Bonus Army marchers were actually veterans. The press criticized MacArthur because of this incident. Some congressmen thought he should resign as Chief of Staff. But other army officials and President Hoover supported him.

War Clouds Gather

On a trip to Europe in 1932, MacArthur realized that many of the European powers were preparing for war. He saw oxcarts bringing supplies for troops in Yugoslavia. Turkey's leader, Mustapha Kemal Ataturk, was desperately trying to replace old equipment. In Czechoslovakia, MacArthur learned, many plants were being built.

MacArthur reported to the American secretary of war that war seemed very likely to break out in Europe. MacArthur also pointed out that a new war would be won by "maneuver and movement."[15] The air force would be especially important, both to attack the enemy and to protect the army and the navy. Congress, however, refused to spend any additional funds for the military at that time.

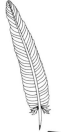

MacArthur's handling of the Bonus Army protest was considered too violent and aggressive by many Americans.

The Civilian Conservation Corps

MacArthur remained Army Chief of Staff after the next presidential election, in which Democrat Franklin Delano Roosevelt defeated Republican President Herbert Hoover. When Roosevelt was inaugurated in March 1933, MacArthur led the inaugural parade on a huge stallion.

Roosevelt's major goal was to help Americans find relief from the Depression. He created what historians call the New Deal, a series of programs designed to get the nation back on its feet.

On March 31, 1933, Congress created the Civilian Conservation Corps (CCC). This program would put five hundred thousand young men to work in the nation's Forest Service, doing work such as planting new trees and constructing park buildings. The army was put in charge of enrolling new recruits, training them, and taking them to work camps.

As Chief of Staff, Douglas MacArthur played an important role in getting the CCC up and running. The army had helped build 1,330 work camps in 47 states. The president was delighted with how smoothly the program got started.

In his capacity as Army Chief of Staff, MacArthur would remain involved with the CCC for two more years. But other matters would soon occupy his attention as well.

6

WORLD WAR II

As Army Chief of Staff, Douglas MacArthur spent a lot of time thinking about what military preparations the United States needed to make. He mounted a campaign to build up the United States Army. Some members of the public and government officials criticized him for doing so. In the early 1930s, most Americans simply could not believe they would see another war in their lifetime. The United States had decided to isolate itself from the problems of other nations. It wanted to maintain a position of neutrality in world affairs, siding with no one.

As Chief of Staff, Douglas MacArthur also considered what weapons the army would need in the future. Even when the army budget was cut during the Great

Depression, he continued to think about new weapons. He put army funds into developing prototypes— experimental weapons—to test. One of his most important achievements was the formation of the Army Air Corps, whose members were all pilots. The army had decided that air power would be very important in the future.

Back to the Philippines

In 1934, MacArthur's term as Chief of Staff was due to expire. President Roosevelt, however, asked him to stay on for another year. His departure in 1935 seemed likely to leave MacArthur in an awkward position. He would no longer be the army's top official. Any new assignment would, in effect, be a demotion. The president solved this problem for him. Franklin Delano Roosevelt asked MacArthur to undertake a special assignment for him, returning to the Philippines as a military advisor. The Philippines had recently become a commonwealth of the United States. This meant the Filipinos governed themselves but the United States was still responsible for the islands' defense and dictated its role in foreign affairs.[1]

MacArthur accepted the job. He and his mother sailed for the Philippines. There, Filipino President Manuel Quezon made MacArthur field marshal of the Filipino Army. This meant he was its highest-ranking officer after the Commander in Chief. As field marshal for five years, MacArthur oversaw the buildup of the Philippine Army.

Douglas MacArthur (left) served as a military advisor to President Franklin Roosevelt (right).

The strengthening of the army had become crucial. In the 1930s, Italy and Germany had begun a military buildup in Europe. In the Far East, Japan also became aggressive, threatening its neighbors. Japan was in the middle of a campaign of expansion, adding territory to its empire. The Philippines needed to prepare to fend off an invasion. Military men like MacArthur saw war clouds looming on two fronts, in Europe and in Asia. Most of the American public continued to believe that their country could remain uninvolved, isolated as it was by two oceans.

A New Romance

In the meantime, Douglas MacArthur experienced huge changes in his personal life. In her old age, his mother was frequently ill. After developing a blood clot in her brain, she died in Manila in 1935, at the age of eighty-four. MacArthur was saddened by the loss but relieved to see her suffering come to an end.

MacArthur, however, had a reason to be happy during this period. After the failure of his marriage, he had begun a new romance. On the voyage to the Philippines, he spent a great deal of time with a fellow passenger named Jean Faircloth. She was described as a tiny, lively, rich, single woman.[2] Faircloth took up residence in Manila, where she and MacArthur continued to date. By this time, MacArthur was nearly sixty. Faircloth was thirty-seven. In April 1937, they married while on a trip to New York City. A year later, on February 21, 1938, their son, Arthur MacArthur IV, was born. His father, who was extremely proud, called

MacArthur (center) returned to the Philippines as a military advisor. While there, he married for a second time.

Arthur "the complete center of my thoughts and affection."[3]

Douglas MacArthur resigned from the United States Army's active list in December 1937.[4] He continued on, however, in his position as field marshal of the Philippine Army.

Outbreak of World War II

Through the end of the 1930s, the world edged toward war. Italy, Germany, and Japan all wanted to expand their power. In 1937, the Japanese Army overran parts of China. In 1939, Germany started its planned conquest of Europe, invading Poland. In response, Great Britain and France declared war on Germany. World War II was now under way.

The United States, however, did not enter the war right away. President Roosevelt did not want to send American troops to fight, but he did lend money and supplies to Great Britain and France to help them fight Germany and its allies. Despite the United States' official neutrality, however, the American military prepared to go to war.

In 1941, Douglas MacArthur sent a telegraph to Washington, D.C. It suggested that he come out of retirement and be named commander of all American forces in the Philippines. He wanted to prepare for war.

Far East Commander

On July 27, 1941, President Roosevelt reassigned MacArthur to active duty in the army, appointing him

Douglas MacArthur is seen here with his wife, Jean.

Japan's Role in World War II

By 1931, the government of Japan became interested in military expansion. The Japanese started to occupy Manchuria, a Chinese province. By 1937, Japan had launched a full-scale war against China.

Germany, Italy, and Japan signed treaties of mutual defense. This meant they would fight for one another in the event that they came under attack. For two years after Germany invaded Poland in 1939, the United States negotiated with Japan, trying to avoid war in the Pacific. In the summer of 1941, however, Japan conquered more of Indochina. When Japan bombed Pearl Harbor on December 7, 1941, it did so because it wanted to destroy the United States Pacific fleet, thereby preventing the United States from playing as large a part in the Pacific campaign as it might have done otherwise.

commander of United States forces in the Far East. MacArthur would also command the Filipino forces that would form the bulk of his troops. MacArthur learned of his new assignment by reading about it in the newspaper.

On August 1, the United States publicly said it would defend the Philippines against the Japanese, who had allied with Germany and Italy in the war.

The United States began to send military supplies to the Philippines. Fourteen companies of American soldiers arrived on September 26. However, by December, MacArthur had only 6,083 Americans in his command, and he lacked equipment.

His plans, however, were in place. He had decided to order the American and Filipino soldiers to hold the Philippines' beaches at all cost. He expected Japan to attack the Philippines from the ocean, using ships to land soldiers. MacArthur's soldiers would fight them as they waded to shore.

In making this decision, MacArthur put aside an earlier plan that said that, in the event of an attack, his soldiers would withdraw to the peninsula of Bataan. Instead, MacArthur decided to keep all his men and supplies on the Philippines' main island, Luzon.

Throughout the fall of 1941, the American government tried to negotiate with the Japanese, hoping to prevent war. But by late November, it was apparent that the negotiations were failing. On November 24, all the Pacific commanders received radio messages from Washington, D.C., telling them to be prepared for the Japanese to launch a "surprise aggressive movement in any direction, including an attack on the Philippines or Guam."[5] Even with this warning, Americans were completely unprepared for what happened next.

The Attack on Pearl Harbor

On December 7, 1941, the Japanese shocked the world when they sent airplanes to bomb American battleships anchored in Pearl Harbor, Hawaii. Just after 3:00 A.M., the United States Navy admiral in the Philippines, Tom Hart, got a phone call telling him of a radio message from Honolulu, Hawaii: "AIR RAID ON PEARL HARBOR. THIS IS NO DRILL."[6]

Hart did not tell MacArthur about the message. Half an hour later, an army signalman listening to a California radio station heard the news. Within minutes, someone had called MacArthur. "Pearl Harbor! It should be our strongest point!" he exclaimed.[7]

Soon he got another phone call, this one from Major General Leonard T. Gerow, in Washington, D.C. Official army records of the phone call show that Gerow stated that he would not be surprised if the Philippines soon came under attack. MacArthur was very much aware of how easy it would be for the Japanese to attack Manila next. But MacArthur later remembered that he came away from talking to Gerow believing that the Japanese had "suffered a serious setback" at Pearl Harbor.[8] At any rate, the shock of the news rattled him so completely that he ordered no preparations.

At first, he just sat at home and read his Bible. Then he went to his office. Other military officials gathered there, too. Later, his companions remembered that he looked "gray, ill, and exhausted."[9] At 5:30 A.M., he got a message informing him that the United States had declared war on Japan.

Great Britain, the Soviet Union, and the United States had already put together what was called the Rainbow Five Plan. The plan said that the Allies would fight only a defensive war against Japan until after the defeat of Germany and Italy. When it was first devised, the plan called for the abandonment of the Philippines. Later, the plan was revised to allow for some defense of key Philippine positions.[10] Despite this provision, MacArthur did nothing to prepare for defense. To this day, historians cannot explain why.

American warships remained anchored in bays in the Philippines. There were no anti-aircraft shelters erected at the airfield. Bomber planes—B-17s—were ready for action—but they had no bombs loaded.[11] At 7:15 A.M., thirty-six smaller American planes—P-40s—took off, hoping to stop enemy planes that had been seen on the radar screen. Other planes, called Flying Fortresses, were also ordered into the air, to make it harder for Japanese aircraft to destroy the P-40s. Only at 11:00 A.M. did MacArthur authorize bombing missions for later in the day. The Fortresses then came back to be armed. The P-40s were also recalled for refueling. In the meantime, the Japanese staged minor raids on northern Luzon, the island on which Manila is located.

Bombing of the Philippines

Just before noon, a radar operator in the Philippines sighted blips on his screen, indicating that aircraft were nearby. Two hundred Japanese aircraft were fast approaching the islands. The operator sent messages to Clark Field, where MacArthur's airplanes were based. But static prevented the messages from being understood. The operator also sent messages over telegraph lines to a small machine called a teletypewriter. But nobody read them in time because all the pilots had gone to lunch.

Earlier, MacArthur had ordered all the B-17s to Mindanao, but his aide had moved only seventeen of the thirty-five big bombers. Japanese bombs destroyed all the remaining Flying Fortresses and half of the remaining planes at Clark Field. Within minutes, the American air force was destroyed. Now MacArthur lacked the planes necessary to bomb the Japanese ships that were approaching, loaded with soldiers, ready to invade. Many historians have criticized MacArthur for the disaster at Clark Field, believing he could have prevented it. However, he was never charged or punished for neglecting his duties.

After the bombing, MacArthur knew that Japanese forces were on the way to the Philippines. He did not know, however, where they would land. He suspected that they would land in the Lingayen Gulf, and from there, they would invade Manila. He believed that the Japanese needed to hold the port of Manila before they could try to take over other territory in Southeast Asia.

Some historians believe MacArthur made a terrible mistake at this point. They say he should have ordered all of his two hundred thousand troops to move into the mountains on Luzon's north end and fight the Japanese guerrilla-style. Instead, he committed his troops to trying to protect the capital of Manila, at least for a time.

The Japanese Reach the Philippines

On December 22, 1941, the Japanese fleet arrived in the Philippines. It landed in Lingayen Gulf, just as MacArthur had predicted. Immediately, forty thousand Japanese troops waded to Luzon. MacArthur's troops simply fled.

On December 24, MacArthur ordered Manila to be evacuated. Among the evacuees were his own family, who went to the small island of Corregidor. MacArthur then ordered all the troops he had on Luzon to retreat to the Bataan peninsula. It took until January 1, 1942, for all the American and Filipino soldiers to get across bridges to Bataan. For two days, American infantrymen had prevented Japanese tanks from making their way across those bridges. Now, MacArthur's engineers blew up the bridges.[12]

In the months that followed, MacArthur expected his troops to sit and wait for help to arrive. He knew the United States Navy would soon be on its way.

7

TO AUSTRALIA AND BACK

When Douglas MacArthur withdrew his forces to Bataan in 1941, he thought his troops would hold those positions for six months. He expected the navy to arrive by that time. Its aircraft carriers and bombs would be used to force the Japanese out of the Philippines.

The MacArthur Family on Corregidor

For two months after the American retreat, the MacArthur family lived in a small house on Corregidor Island. It was a sad, scary time for them. Every day, Japanese bombs hit the island.

MacArthur's wife, Jean; his three-year-old son, Arthur; and Arthur's nanny, a Chinese woman named Ah Chuh, had to spend almost all their time indoors.

Like MacArthur's men, they ate horsemeat for lack of other food. Because he was the commander, MacArthur's family had some canned goods that ordinary soldiers could not get, but they had no fresh vegetables or milk. And they quickly ran out of ways to pass the time without boredom.[1]

Headquarters

Douglas MacArthur set up his military headquarters in a tunnel cut deep into Corregidor Island. During air raids, everybody on Corregidor fled to the tunnel— except for MacArthur, who stood outside and watched the bombs fall. Always a risk taker, he never even wore a helmet.[2]

MacArthur's troops were mainly stationed on Bataan. There, they dug a line of foxholes, shallow pits into which they jumped whenever bombing started. They lived out in the open, without much water. Soon they were starving and filthy.

MacArthur worried about the men on Bataan, but he visited them only once in the seventy-seven days he spent on Corregidor. Historian Jules Archer explained that MacArthur wanted to set up another command station on Bataan but changed his mind when Filipino President Manuel Quezon protested, saying MacArthur's life would be in much greater danger on Bataan. If MacArthur died, Quezon warned, the Filipino people might agree to join the Japanese Empire. Quezon believed that the Filipinos were loyal to MacArthur, but not the United States. Japanese airplanes had been dropping messages for the Filipinos, promising them that, if they joined Japan, they could soon have independence. Quezon was afraid they might believe the promise. So MacArthur stayed on Corregidor. Some of his men nicknamed him Dugout Doug. They thought he was a coward.[3]

Historian William Manchester described MacArthur and his men as being "caught in a gigantic trap—the largest trap in the history of warfare."[4] On January 9, the Japanese attacked Bataan. Six days later, MacArthur was urging his troops to fight on, telling them they would soon be reinforced.

The Japanese bombed Corregidor, too. The Filipino people were becoming discouraged. On February 8, Filipino President Manuel Quezon sent a message to American President Franklin Delano Roosevelt, asking him to grant the Philippines immediate independence so that it might adopt a neutral stance in the war and have both the American and the Japanese troops leave. Roosevelt refused. He did not want the Japanese to see the United States as weak. He did, however, send new messages to MacArthur, informing him that ships carrying new troops were en route and authorizing him to surrender.[5] President Roosevelt suggested that Quezon and other Filipino political leaders fly to Australia.

Escape

On February 16, MacArthur ordered his troops to assault the enemy once again. Still, the Japanese continued to press forward. On February 22, MacArthur

Bataan Death March

The Bataan Death March was one of the grimmest events in World War II. After Douglas MacArthur left Corregidor, the Japanese began an intensive bombing of Bataan on March 24, 1942. Bitter ground fighting followed. On April 9, the Allied forces on Bataan were forced to surrender.

The Japanese took seventy thousand Filipino and American prisoners of war. They forced these POWs to march sixty-five miles under hot sun, denying them virtually all food and water. Many prisoners who fell along the way were bayoneted. Only fifty-four thousand prisoners made it to the camp where they were to be imprisoned. As many as ten thousand had died on the way. (Approximately ten thousand more had escaped.) Many thousands more POWs died in the camp.

received orders to leave Corregidor for Mindanao, a more isolated island in the Philippines. From there, he could go to Australia to take command of all Allied troops in the Pacific.

At first, MacArthur decided to disobey these orders. Instead, he wanted to resign his position as an officer, reenlist in the army as a soldier, and fight beside his men on Bataan. His staff officers persuaded him not to.

The Pacific War

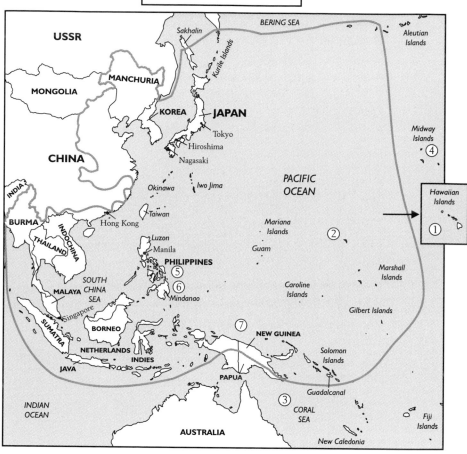

Key to Air and Naval Battles:

① Pearl Harbor ④ Midway ⑦ Bismarck Sea

② Wake Island ⑤ Philippine Sea

③ Coral Sea ⑥ Leyte Gulf

Limit of Japanese Expansion

The Philippines were at the center of the war in the Pacific.

A submarine was scheduled to pick up MacArthur and his family and staff on March 15. But on March 9, a lull occurred in the fighting on Bataan. There had been a change in leadership in the Japanese Army. On March 12, MacArthur, his family, their nanny, and his aides boarded PT boats. They all suffered during the two days it took to reach Mindanao.[6] The boats tossed in the turbulent sea. Douglas MacArthur got seasick, and his son was sick with a fever.[7]

When MacArthur left the Philippines, General Jonathan Wainwright took command of his troops. The American and Filipino soldiers who were left behind continued to fight. But on May 6, Wainwright was forced to surrender to Japanese forces. The Japanese then took approximately one hundred forty thousand soldiers prisoner throughout the Philippines.[8] The prisoners would suffer terribly.

A New Command

On March 17, MacArthur reached Australia. By this time, the American troops who had been left in the

PT Boats
PT—patrol torpedo—boats were some of the smallest, fastest, and easiest-to-maneuver fighting ships of the navy. Nicknamed mosquito boats because they "stung" the enemy with great speed, they were equipped with four torpedo tubes and four machine guns.

Philippines generally spoke poorly of MacArthur. They felt he had abandoned them. However, his reputation in the United States remained untarnished. In fact, Congress awarded him the Congressional Medal of Honor for his gallant efforts in the Philippines.[9]

During his flight to Australia, the Allies had agreed to reorganize their command in the Far East. The British had taken responsibility for fighting in the Indian Ocean and the Middle East. The American Joint Chiefs of Staff now directed all Pacific operations. Fighting in Europe was overseen by American and British commanders. MacArthur was appointed commander of all Allied forces in the southwest Pacific.

Fighting From Australia

Following his arrival in Australia, MacArthur prepared for a Japanese invasion of Australia. At that point, the Japanese hoped to arrive in Port Moresby, on the island of New Guinea, located just north of Australia. If they could land there, they could then send troops to take Australia. On May 5 to 8, 1942, American and Japanese ships fought near New Guinea. The Japanese finally retreated. But it remained to be seen if they would come back. MacArthur continued to prepare for an attack.

The Allies then achieved a very important victory. The American navy had been using Midway Island, located in the central Pacific Ocean, as a supply base. The Japanese Navy decided to stage a surprise attack on the base. If it were destroyed, the United States

Navy would have to leave the Pacific. But codebreakers deciphered the code that Japanese ships used to send messages, so the Americans knew about the plans. From June 3 to 6, 1942, American dive-bombers attacked the Japanese fleet as it headed toward Midway, sinking four aircraft carriers and destroying hundreds of planes.

The American victory at the Battle of Midway encouraged General George C. Marshall, the United States Army Chief of Staff, to send more men and supplies to the Pacific.[10] Navy Admiral Chester W. Nimitz began to lay plans to attack Japan from Hawaii. At the same time, MacArthur prepared to attack from the south. President Roosevelt wanted to create competition between the army and the navy—to see who would reach Japan first.

By July, the United States had a new Pacific policy. The first objective was to seize territory around New Guinea.[11] MacArthur began to fortify New Guinea. The Japanese had seized Rabaul, on New Britain, just northeast of New Guinea. In August, the Japanese pressed forward into New Guinea, but MacArthur's troops fought back and won. This was the first time in World War II that the Allies had beaten the Japanese on land.

MacArthur then launched an all-out offensive on New Guinea. Finally, in January 1943, the Allies took the last Japanese stronghold on the island. MacArthur's men had become sick and exhausted fighting through its hot, steamy jungle, but they had ultimately triumphed. Now the Allies could start to push Japan even farther back.

Throughout this long period, Jean and Arthur MacArthur lived in Brisbane, Australia. The general lived on military posts in Australia and later in New Guinea. Every once in a while, he could visit his family, but it was a lonely and frightening time for them. Arthur MacArthur, born in the Philippines, had never even been to the United States.

Meeting With Roosevelt

By the spring of 1943, it appeared that the Allies would soon win the war in Europe. But the outcome in the Pacific was much less certain. MacArthur's main goal was to take back the Philippines from Japan. Slowly, the Allies fought their way north, from island to island, forcing the Japanese to abandon territory they had seized. By the summer of 1944, MacArthur and his soldiers had fought back two thousand miles and sat within three hundred miles of the Philippines.[12]

In July 1944, MacArthur—commander of the soldiers in the Pacific—and Navy Admiral Chester Nimitz—commander of the sailors there—met with President Roosevelt in Honolulu, Hawaii, to discuss strategy. Spies had learned that the Japanese were sending new troops into the western Pacific. The Joint Chiefs of Staff thought that the Allies should attack Japan directly. They wanted to launch an attack from Formosa, the island just east of China that is called Taiwan today. But MacArthur persuaded Roosevelt that a direct assault on Taiwan would result in many

Allied deaths. The attack, he insisted, should come from the Philippines.[13]

Return to the Philippines

In September 1944, the United States had 1.5 million soldiers and marines fighting on islands in the Pacific. The navy had also sent all its biggest aircraft carriers there. There were not only many ships, but also planes in the area.

MacArthur's forces landed in the Molucca Islands, close to the Philippines, in September 1944. From October 12 to 16, American ships launched air attacks on Taiwan and Luzon. These attacks, they hoped, would make it easier to land troops on Leyte, a smaller Philippine island. On October 14, American troops boarded ships for Leyte. Six days later, the invasion force landed.[14] MacArthur had returned to the Philippines.

Under his direction of the Battle of Leyte Gulf on October 23 to 26, the Japanese suffered defeat. Later, Emperor Hirohito of Japan told MacArthur that it was the defeat on Leyte that convinced him Japan had lost the war. American planes dropped so many bombs that the Japanese Navy had no aircraft carriers left when the battle ended. They had all sunk.

The Japanese offered so much resistance on Leyte that MacArthur delayed the landings he had planned for Luzon from December 20, 1944, to January 9, 1945. At first, the United States met no opposition when it landed in the Lingayen Gulf on Luzon. But fierce fighting took place when American troops tried to continue inland. On January 26, Americans finally reached Clark Field. American troops cleared all Japanese resistance from Manila by March 3. During fighting in the capital, residents suffered terribly. Their city was virtually destroyed.

Once Manila was back in his hands, Douglas MacArthur sent for Jean and Arthur. His wife and son took a ship from Brisbane back to the Philippines. Reunited, the MacArthurs moved into a house in Manila's suburbs.

The defeat of the Japanese at the Battle of Leyte Gulf was a major turning point in the war in the Pacific.

The Atomic Bomb

While MacArthur and his command fought in the Philippines, the navy also attacked the Japanese on Iwo Jima, an island seven hundred miles from Japan, in late January 1945. It took the Allied forces six weeks to achieve victory there.

Then, American troops landed on Okinawa, only three hundred fifty miles from Japan. The Japanese fought hard there, too, but again the Allies won. On April 3, 1945, Nimitz and MacArthur received orders to make plans to invade Japan. However, they would never have to use them.

Scientists for the last few years had been secretly working on a new weapon for the United States—the atomic bomb. Military officials first tested the bomb in July 1945. It had far more destructive power than any weapon invented earlier. When new President Harry Truman found out that the atomic bomb worked, he warned Japan that it must surrender or face "prompt and utter destruction."[15]

Hoping to save lives by defeating Japan with one decisive attack, on August 6, 1945, the United States dropped an atomic bomb on Hiroshima, Japan. The bomb killed eighty thousand people immediately. Another thirty-seven thousand suffered hideous injuries. Every building in forty-two square miles was destroyed.

On August 9, a second atomic bomb was dropped on another Japanese city, Nagasaki. This attack resulted in another thirty-five thousand deaths.[16] The same day,

Hirohito (right), the emperor of Japan during World War II, credited MacArthur's success in the Pacific with convincing him the war was hopeless. Hirohito made the decision to surrender in August 1945.

Soviet troops invaded Manchuria, signaling the Soviet Union's declaration of war on Japan.

Most members of the Supreme Council, which governed Japan, agreed that Japan had to surrender.[17] The council's military members, however, wanted to keep fighting. The decision fell to Japanese Emperor Hirohito. On August 15, Hirohito broadcast a radio message. In it, he informed his people of the country's surrender.

Following the surrender, MacArthur was named Supreme Allied Commander. On August 30, he landed in Japan. MacArthur's popularity among Americans was stronger than ever. A poll ranked him second only to General Dwight D. Eisenhower among American heroes.[18]

The Japanese Surrender

On April 30, 1945, German dictator Adolf Hitler had committed suicide when he realized that his country had lost to the Allies. American and Soviet troops had already marched into Germany, which surrendered on May 8, ending the war in Europe.

On September 2, 1945, the Japanese formally surrendered to MacArthur—in his position as Supreme Commander—on the American battleship *Missouri* in Tokyo Bay. On September 8, MacArthur arrived in Tokyo. He immediately sent for his wife and child.

On September 22, he set up an international war tribunal to try those accused of war crimes in Japan. The trial lasted from June 3, 1946, to November 4, 1948. At its conclusion, twenty-five of the twenty-eight high Japanese officials accused of war crimes were found guilty. Seven were hanged on December 23, 1948. The others were imprisoned.

Occupation of Japan

MacArthur served as military ruler of Japan, which was occupied by the Allies, until 1950. In this role, he acted with good will. Some American officials wanted to punish the Japanese. MacArthur, however, resisted. He did not want revenge for the United States, even though the war had cost an enormous amount of money and lives. Instead, he offered the Japanese, in

After World War II, MacArthur was placed in charge of Japan as its military ruler. He worked to establish a democracy there. He is seen here signing the Japanese articles of surrender.

his own words, "the solace and hope and faith of Christian morals."[19]

After the surrender, the Japanese people suffered terribly from *ensei*—the Japanese word for weariness of living.[20] The country was devastated. Before the war, it had been a great center of industry. Now bombs had destroyed many of its cities. After the war, Japan had no power plants. The nation needed 4 million new houses. MacArthur found himself in charge of a country that lacked even basic necessities such as food.

Biographer Sydney Mayer wrote that MacArthur's reconstruction of postwar Japan was one of his greatest achievements.[21] Throughout his term there, he followed his conscience. He had never received orders to establish democracy in Japan. He had just been told to restore order. Nevertheless, democracy was his goal. He issued orders granting the Japanese people political and religious freedom. He made sure that the newspapers could print whatever they wanted. He also called for a new constitution for the country and drafted much of it himself.[22] In 1947, a new constitution was adopted in Japan. It provided for the establishment of a democratic government.

In the meantime, the Philippines became independent of the United States on July 4, 1946. The new government there was immediately challenged by a militant movement of the people. This dismayed MacArthur. He had hoped that the land he loved could experience peace and prosperity. Although no one knew it then, the Far East would remain in great turmoil for decades. MacArthur would be needed in the area for a long time to come.

8

KOREA

In the early twentieth century, political leader Vladimir Lenin established a new, Communist form of government in Russia, which became the Soviet Union after the Bolshevik Revolution of 1917. The goal of communism is for all the people in a country to share wealth and property equally. After World War II, Communists—people who support this type of government—gained power in Asia and parts of Europe. They aimed to overthrow the existing governments.

Communism in Japan
In Japan, Douglas MacArthur saw Communist uprisings. Upholding Japanese freedom, he had actually granted the Communist party the right to exist in

Japan, and had chosen not to censor a Communist newspaper there.[1] In January 1948, however, the Communist party organized a general strike—it asked workers to walk off the job. MacArthur stepped in. He warned the public that this would lead to the shutdown of transportation, would stop food deliveries, and would cause industry to collapse. The government then banned strikes by government employees, censored

MacArthur for President

In the fall of 1947, MacArthur began to let American visitors to Japan know that he would like to run for president on the Republican ticket in the next election. Later, he claimed that he had never campaigned, but this was not true.

By February 1948, journalists knew that the Midwestern vote would determine the Republican nomination. This was good news for MacArthur because that was where most of his support was.[2] However, in the primaries, he failed to win many delegates. Many of his supporters thought he should come home to the United States if he wanted to run for president. Had he wanted to go on, he would have had to resign from the army, because officers serving in the military cannot participate in politics. He clearly did not want to resign his commission. In the spring, he asked that his name be removed from primary tickets. He seemed to have no chance of winning.[3]

the Communist newspaper, and refused to let many Japanese visit Communist countries.[4]

Communism also failed to gain more ground in Japan because MacArthur helped Japanese industry recover and worked for land reform.[5] For centuries, only feudal lords could own land in Japan. These extremely rich men divided their property into tiny farms that they rented out to the people. The poor tenant farmers had to give the lords a share of their crops. MacArthur changed the system to allow farmers to buy the land they worked at low prices and pay for it over a long period of time. Tenant farmers then bought 5 million acres, almost 90 percent of the country's farmland. It made MacArthur very proud to have created a more equal society for Japan.[6]

The Cold War Begins

The Soviet Union and the United States had been allies during World War II. But relations between the two countries fell apart after the war as Joseph Stalin, the Soviet dictator, tried to extend his country's power through Eastern Europe and Asia. The Cold War, which would pit Americans and their allies against the Soviets and their Communist allies, began in 1945. Outright war never broke out, but the United States and the Soviet Union built up their supplies of arms, including nuclear weapons, to be ready for battle if necessary.

The United States wanted to contain Soviet influence. By 1949, communism had already begun to spread. Communist armies led by Mao Tse-tung took over China and established the Communist People's Republic of China. The old ruler, Chinese Nationalist leader Chiang Kai-shek, fled to Taiwan, where he set up a government that would fight against Red, or Communist, China, for legitimacy.

MacArthur had predicted that Communists would soon hold important bases all over Asia.[7] President Harry Truman and other officials concluded that the United States had to build up its military to prevent further Communist expansion. A much larger army was needed. Americans felt fear when they learned the Soviets had their own atomic bombs in September 1949. Congress agreed it needed to spend much more money to keep communism in check.

The Creation of Korea

In the meantime, MacArthur withdrew the last American troops from Korea, a peninsula in eastern Asia, in the summer of 1949. Until the end of World War II, Korea had been part of the Japanese Empire. After the war, the United States and the Soviet Union occupied Korea jointly. The Soviet Union occupied Korea above the 38th parallel of latitude, setting up a Communist government. The United States, on the other hand, supported a democratic (although corrupt) government in the area it occupied below the parallel. In August 1948, MacArthur visited Seoul, South Korea, for the inauguration of the country's president, Syngman Rhee. In January 1949, the Soviets announced the withdrawal of all their troops from North Korea. At one point, the United States had wanted to help the two parts of Korea be reunited into a single country. But President Truman had finally decided that this was up to the United Nations, the world peace-keeping organization founded in 1945.

North Korea Invades South Korea

There would be no peaceful reunion. On June 25, 1950, North Korea invaded South Korea. Although military officials had considered an invasion possible, most Americans were completely surprised. Many did not even know where Korea was.[8]

President Truman believed Soviet leader Joseph Stalin was behind the invasion of South Korea. Truman thought Stalin wanted to find out whether the United States would actually put up a fight to prevent communism from spreading farther. Truman asked the United Nations (UN) to send troops to fight on behalf of South Korea. The UN agreed. Plans were made to send soldiers and weapons. United States armed troops would make up the majority of the UN forces.[9]

The American Response

Truman and his advisors decided that Douglas MacArthur should command the UN troops that would fight. MacArthur accepted. At first, he expected the Korean War to be a short conflict.

On June 25, 1950, officials in Washington, D.C., sent him his first orders. He received control over all members of the United States Army and Navy in and around Asia. He was also instructed to support the

Republic of Korea and he was given the new title of American Commander in Chief, Far East. On July 14, in a ceremony in Tokyo, MacArthur also became the first commander of a United Nations Army.[10] He now saw himself first and foremost as an international officer, one who would answer not to the United States president, but to the United Nations.

At first, MacArthur hoped that airplanes and ships alone could help South Korean troops drive the North Koreans out of their territory. But he soon realized he was going to have to send soldiers, too. Infantry would be needed to protect any airstrips Americans secured.

Americans' Fear of Communism

During the Korean War, many Americans expressed a deep fear of communism. In 1950, Republican Senator Joseph R. McCarthy began a campaign to rid the United States of the Communists he suspected were everywhere. He gave many speeches, warning of the presence of Communists in high positions in the United States government. Many people were investigated for their political beliefs, and some lost their jobs because of suspected Communist beliefs. For a time, McCarthy was extremely popular for making strong attacks on Communists. Eventually, however, when he tried to expose Communists in the army, people realized his methods were unfair and often ridiculous. McCarthy and the anti-Communist movement he helped begin soon lost support.

MacArthur visited the battlefront for the first time on June 29, 1950. He spent eight dangerous hours touring South Korea's army lines. All day he watched crowds of refugees—South Korean residents fleeing from the North Korean invaders—swarm around the disorganized South Korean Army.[11] Earlier, South Korean soldiers had destroyed bridges crossing the Han, one of their country's northern rivers, to make it harder for North Korean soldiers to push farther south. Hundreds of refugees who were crossing the bridges at that time were killed. The lack of bridges also left a large number of South Korean troops stranded on the north side of the river.

Back in Japan that evening, MacArthur telephoned Washington, D.C. Word of what he had seen that day was passed on to the president. The next morning, Truman announced that, in addition to authorizing air force missions in North Korea and the naval blockade of the entire Korean coast, MacArthur would be using ground units.

Inchon

At first, UN forces had little success in the Korean War. But then, MacArthur got approval for an amphibious (water to land) landing in the harbor of Inchon. For a long time, he had been reluctant to tell Washington, D.C., fully about his plans. When he finally told his plan to Navy Rear Admiral James Doyle, Doyle was struck dumb. There was no beach at Inchon. The invaders would have to come from the water over piers and seawalls directly into a city. Dangerous currents ran through the bay, which Doyle suspected was already mined by the enemy. The Joint Chiefs of Staff, upon learning that MacArthur had selected Inchon as his target, sent two staff members to try and talk him out of it. But he presented his case forcefully. He pointed out that surprise was the best of all weapons. He argued that the navy could help him overcome the obstacles Inchon represented. From Inchon, he pointed out, he could easily take back Seoul, the capital of South Korea. This would cut off the enemy's supply lines. Four days later, the Chiefs of Staff agreed to his plan.[12]

MacArthur had arrived back in the Philippines during World War II with an amphibious landing. He hoped to repeat his success at Inchon.

On Wednesday, September 13, four huge American aircraft carriers entered Inchon Harbor. Smaller warships, called destroyers, followed. Warplanes took off from the carriers and bombed the enemy. The next night, 261 ships from seven nations arrived in the harbor, too. On September 15, at 5:40 A.M., American guns signaled that it was time for the landing force to go ashore.

At first, MacArthur just watched from the bow of his ship. When the tide went out, he boarded a barge. He had hoped to go ashore then, too. However, he soon realized that it would be possible for a sniper to shoot him while he waded to shore, and he gave up the idea. He went ashore on Sunday, after Inchon had been captured.

The cost of the victory for the UN troops was relatively small. Out of thousands of soldiers, only 536 had died. Twenty-five hundred had been wounded. The UN troops had overcome a force of between thirty thousand and forty thousand.[13]

MacArthur rejoiced at his victory. One army officer, however, tried to warn him that all was not well. James M. Gavin, an American military official, noticed that North Korea had prepared Kimpo Airfield to be used by a large, modern air force. The North Koreans expected backup from the Communist Chinese, Gavin concluded.

MacArthur's amphibious landing at Inchon surprised the enemy and helped him cut North Korea's supply lines.

Gavin explained his worries to Charles Willoughby, MacArthur's intelligence chief. Willoughby thought Gavin was being foolish. He argued that, if the Chinese meant to intervene, they would have done so during the Inchon landing. MacArthur had taken the Chinese by surprise with the speedy Inchon landing, Gavin replied. Despite Gavin's arguments, Willoughby remained convinced that the Communist Chinese would stay out of the Korean War.[14]

On September 26, the city of Seoul fell to the Americans. In the meantime, other American soldiers had marched to Suwon. Now half the North Korean troops were trapped between two American flanks. Those who were not killed fled for the 38th parallel. During North Korea's three-month invasion, many South Korean people had been killed and many others had lost their homes. Then, in fifteen days, MacArthur had freed South Korea from the Communists.

9

ALONG THE
38TH
PARALLEL

At first, after MacArthur's troops forced the Communists out of South Korea, military action stopped. At the end of September 1950, MacArthur flew back to Japan, where he picked up his wife, Jean, so she could go with him back to Korea for a while. There, MacArthur oversaw ceremonies reinstating Syngman Rhee as head of the Republic of Korea. In doing so, he went against the wishes of the United States government, which had informed him he could not do so without "approval of higher authority."[1]

At this point, the future of Korea was being debated in the United Nations. Initially, the United States and its allies wanted only to push the North Koreans out of South Korea. Now, members of the United Nations were considering going further. Some wanted to push the North Koreans out of South Korea and then take the war into North Korea, hoping to defeat the Communists in their own territory. Then North and South Korea could reunite and form a single, democratic nation. On the day of the Inchon landing, the American Joint Chiefs of Staff had told MacArthur to draw up plans for the possible occupation of North Korea.

North of the 38th Parallel

On September 27, MacArthur received orders to "conduct military operations north of the 38th Parallel" and aim for "the destruction of the North Korean armed forces."[2] He was told not to allow American airplanes to fly over Chinese or Soviet territory. He could send only South Korean troops (not soldiers from the United States or any other allied country) as far as the Yalu River, which was the border between North Korea and Manchuria. With these exceptions, he could take any action he thought necessary. MacArthur, however, wanted clearer instructions.

On October 2, he received a new message from American Secretary of Defense George Marshall. This one told MacArthur to proceed, but not to inform the American government of his actions. American officials hoped that MacArthur would cross the 38th parallel and successfully force the Communist North Koreans to surrender. Then, the Americans could inform their allies in the United Nations of the new military action.

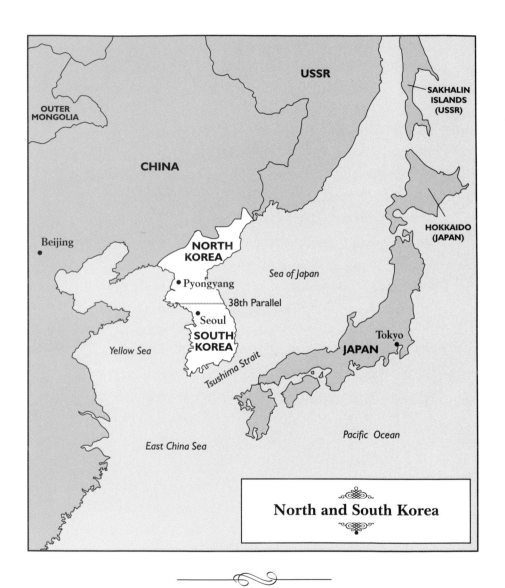

After World War II, Korea was divided between Communist and non-Communist governments at the 38th parallel.

MacArthur now considered his orders definite. On October 7, the matter was settled. The General Assembly of the United Nations voted 47 to 5 to adopt as its objective the creation of a "unified, independent and democratic government" to rule all of Korea.[3]

The Chinese Get Involved

When the Chinese government found out about MacArthur's troops' moving toward China's border and the United Nations' desire to see Korea unified, it decided that China was in danger. The Chinese foreign minister, Chou En-lai, had already issued public warnings that, if MacArthur's forces crossed the 38th parallel, the Chinese Army "would not stand aside."[4]

After MacArthur received orders from the United Nations to try to unify Korea, he asked North Korea's top leader, or premier, to surrender. North Korean Premier Kim Il Sung made no reply, but Chou En-lai did. He said the Americans were threatening Chinese security. That afternoon, Chinese troops began to cross into North Korea. MacArthur and his troops, however, knew nothing of the Chinese military buildup.

The Meeting With Truman

By October 12, American troops had gone as far into North Korea as MacArthur was allowed to send them. He was allowed to send only South Korean soldiers if he wished to go farther. American military officials hoped this would help stop the war from becoming a conflict between the United States and the Soviet Union and China.

That day, MacArthur received a cable from Secretary of Defense George Marshall. It told him that President Truman wanted to meet with him face-to-face on October 15. MacArthur agreed to meet Truman on Wake Island, a tiny island in the southern Pacific Ocean.

To this day, historians are not sure why President Truman wanted to speak to MacArthur. At that point, Truman was unpopular with many Americans. Because Congress never officially declared war on North Korea, he—as Commander in Chief—was seen as being in charge of the war, which was dragging on far longer than the American public had expected or wanted.[5] MacArthur's officers suggested that Truman wanted to bolster his popularity by being seen with MacArthur, who had achieved so many recent victories. Coverage of the meeting by newspapers and radio might help convince Americans to vote for Truman's fellow Democrats in the next congressional elections, scheduled to take place in just three weeks. Publicly, MacArthur said he thought Truman just wanted to create good will. In private, however, he said he thought Truman was making a "political junket," or using the meeting for political advantage.[6]

According to historian William Manchester, MacArthur arrived on Wake Island before Truman and went to the air field to meet him.[7] The two had never met before.[8] After having their pictures taken, they went off alone to talk for half an hour.

There is no record of what they said. Apparently, they talked about the military strength of the United States and its allies. MacArthur probably explained his plans to release an army division from duty in Japan early the next year.

Then they went back to the main meeting, which MacArthur's staff and presidential advisors also attended. As a group, they discussed matters including how much aid Korea would need before the end of the war and MacArthur's progress in making a new Japanese peace treaty. This treaty, which would go into effect after the American occupation of Japan ended, would govern future relations between the two nations.

Toward the end of the meeting, they talked about whether the Soviet Union or China might intervene in the war in Korea. MacArthur told Truman he did not expect either Communist country to do so. He said there were not enough Soviet troops nearby to be a threat. He did acknowledge that Soviet planes could fight in

Many believed Truman tried to connect himself with MacArthur to hide his unpopularity as president behind MacArthur's military fame, as depicted in this political cartoon.

Truman (left) and MacArthur met on Wake Island to discuss the Korean conflict.

partnership with Chinese ground troops. He then went on to discuss the possibility of Chinese intervention without Soviet backup. According to MacArthur, Chinese leader Mao had only fifty thousand troops that could cross the Yalu (one hundred eighty thousand Chinese soldiers would actually cross the river). He also said that Mao had no air force.

All remarks made at this meeting were recorded, without MacArthur's knowledge, by Vernice Anderson, a secretary who was sitting in an adjacent room. Anderson herself told reporters that, when the meeting began, although no one had told her to—or not to—she "automatically" started writing. "It seemed the thing to do," she said.[9]

The meeting between Truman and MacArthur ended after Truman decorated MacArthur with his fifth Distinguished Service Medal. Truman complimented MacArthur on "his vision, his judgment, his indomitable will and his unshakeable faith. . . ."[10] Truman and his advisors then departed in the only available cars, leaving MacArthur to hitchhike back to the air field.

After the Meeting

Back in Washington, D.C., White House representative Stewart Alsop told reporters that MacArthur had told Truman that the Chinese could not possibly intervene in Korea. Asked by a publisher whether he had said this, MacArthur simply replied, "The statement from Stewart Alsop . . . is entirely without foundation in fact."[11] (MacArthur did not know that Vernice

Anderson had taken notes of what took place during the meeting and had recorded his saying otherwise.)

In the fall of 1950, the tide began to turn against the United States in the Korean War. MacArthur complained that a spy was telling the Communists everything he intended to do. United States government officials did not believe him. Historians have since concluded, however, that he may have been right. Copies of all MacArthur's messages concerning Korea went to the British government, which had troops fighting in Korea. Years later, it was discovered that two members of the British Embassy in the United States and the head of Great Britain's American Department were spies working for the Soviet Union.[12] It seems possible that they betrayed MacArthur and his troops.

In late October, under MacArthur's orders, the UN troops continued to advance. His X Corps planned to advance in amphibious maneuvers toward the Yalu River from the right. The Eighth Army would attack from the left, and the South Koreans would continue to hold the center. MacArthur wanted to pin the North Korean Army along the Yalu River. He thought the war was as good as won. He told the United States government he needed no more reinforcements.

Then, on October 24, he ordered X Corps and the 8th Army to drive forward to the Yalu. In doing so, he went against orders he had received earlier from American Secretary of Defense George Marshall, which forbade him to send any non-Koreans into that region. The United States government questioned his decision but did not tell him to stop. MacArthur, in turn, told them he had discussed this move with the president on Wake Island.

A Trap

In late October, MacArthur's troops encountered Chinese for the first time. Soon he realized he might be about to fall into a trap. He ordered the bombing of Yalu bridges by ninety planes. The American Joint Chiefs of Staff wired MacArthur, ordering him to postpone this bombing. He agreed but told them that Chinese troops were pouring across the Yalu. They continued to argue over the matter, and President Truman became involved.

The Chinese then disappeared. Suddenly, in late November, they reappeared. Fierce fighting followed. The Americans began to suffer losses. Altogether MacArthur lost 12,975 men. The Chinese now had more troops than the United Nations forces. At this point, the White House reversed its Korean policy. No longer did Truman or his advisors want MacArthur to try to unite Korea.[13] They feared that, if the UN troops fought on, a third world war might erupt, with China and the Soviet Union allied against the United States, Great Britain, and their allies. Truman was willing to let the Communists stay in North Korea, as long as they left South Korea alone.

MacArthur Wants to Go After China

MacArthur pulled his troops back into South Korea, but he continued to tell his superiors that he thought the United Nations should attack China. In late December, General Matthew B. Ridgway became the new field commander in Korea, commanding all UN ground forces. MacArthur remained the Supreme Commander, Ridgway's superior.

Ridgway strengthened the United Nations' position, gaining a little ground without heavy losses. At the same time, he began to demonstrate that MacArthur was not as essential as everyone had thought. MacArthur asked his superiors in Washington, D.C., for permission to bomb either a target in Manchuria or a Chinese supply depot in North Korea. Permission was denied.[14] American military officials still did not want to fight the Chinese directly.

As 1951 began, United Nations soldiers began to lose serious ground. The North Korean Army, which included thousands of Chinese volunteers, recaptured Seoul. MacArthur had already been given orders to withdraw to Japan if necessary. In January, he received a personal letter from President Truman. It said, "we must act with great prudence so far as extending the area of hostilities. . . ."[15] MacArthur thought the letter meant that Truman wanted him to fight until he conquered the enemy. This was a grave misunderstanding of the intentions of Truman, who had begun to realize that it might be too risky for the United Nations to try to win the war.

By the end of February 1951, the Americans were once again advancing. In late March, the Truman administration drew up a statement, which said that the United Nations wanted to end the war. MacArthur got a copy before it was sent out. On March 24, he issued to the press what he called a "military appraisal." It was basically an ultimatum: Communist China should either submit to his forces or face "imminent military collapse."[16] In issuing this statement, MacArthur drastically overstepped his boundaries.

MacArthur Is Fired

It was still March 23, 1951, in Washington, D.C., when word arrived of MacArthur's public warnings to the Chinese. Immediately, senior government officials gathered to discuss the problem. They all agreed that MacArthur had to be fired, outright. He had disobeyed orders and made an independent, unauthorized declaration concerning foreign policy. He had ignored the authority of both the president and the United Nations.

The matter was finally settled on April 11, 1951. President Truman stripped General MacArthur of all commands. The news was reported in newspapers and on the radio before MacArthur himself

President Truman (seen here) fired MacArthur for disobeying the orders of the president and the United Nations.

was formally notified. Listening to the radio, his aide-de-camp, Colonel Sidney Huff, heard that President Truman had issued a public statement in which he said he was replacing MacArthur with Ridgway as Supreme Commander. Huff then telephoned Jean MacArthur. She went to tell her husband the news at an official luncheon he was attending. Supposedly, after she whispered the news to him, he sat, neither speaking nor moving, for a moment or two. Then he looked up at her and said, "Jeannie, we're going home at last."[17]

10

AFTERMATH

In the spring of 1951, Douglas MacArthur and his family made a triumphant return to the United States from Japan. At the time, many Americans supported MacArthur. They thought Truman had fired him unfairly. Even those who agreed that he should no longer command the troops involved in the Korean War questioned the way in which he had been removed from his duties. They felt he should have been allowed to retire. Most historians, however, have generally agreed that Truman was right to fire MacArthur, who had disobeyed the orders of the Commander in Chief.[1]

On April 16, Douglas, Jean, and Arthur MacArthur left Japan. Huge crowds lined the streets to watch them drive to the airport. People held up signs expressing their support for MacArthur and their sorrow over his departure. When MacArthur's plane landed in Hawaii, another crowd turned out to greet him.[2]

Back Home

When the MacArthurs arrived by plane in San Francisco that night, half a million people were out on the streets, hoping to see him. This would be the first time

MacArthur delivered a speech to Congress in which he commented, "Old soldiers never die. They just fade away."

thirteen-year-old Arthur MacArthur had ever been in North America. When the MacArthurs flew into Washington National Airport just after midnight, on April 19, 1951, thousands of people were at the airport, including the Joint Chiefs of Staff, the secretary of defense, and several members of Congress.

MacArthur spent the rest of the night rewriting a speech that he would deliver to the United States Congress on the afternoon of April 19. When he arrived, all the members rose to their feet. During his speech, which lasted thirty-four minutes, congressmen broke into applause many times. He also received thirty standing ovations.

In what has been called his "Old Soldiers Never Die" speech, MacArthur explained, in his view, the history of the Far East and the Korean War. He justified his actions in Korea. At the end, he praised the nation's fighting men, then said,

> I am closing my fifty-two years of military service. When I joined the Army, even before the turn of the century, it was fulfillment of all my boyish hopes and dreams. The world has turned over many times since I took the oath on the Plain at West Point, and the hopes and dreams have long since vanished. But I still remember the refrain of one of the most popular barrack ballads of that day, which proclaimed, most proudly, "Old soldiers never die. They just fade away." And like the soldier of that ballad, I now close my military career and just fade away—an old soldier who tried to do his duty as God gave him the light to see that duty. Good-bye.[3]

This speech was so well-received that members of the president's Cabinet became alarmed, thinking

MacArthur's actions had hurt Truman terribly. They expected the president to become more unpopular than ever.

The MacArthur family moved to New York City. When they checked into the Waldorf Astoria Hotel, they found sacks upon sacks of mail waiting for them—one hundred fifty thousand letters and twenty thousand telegrams. On April 22, there was a parade held in MacArthur's honor. It took MacArthur's car seven hours to cover the nineteen-mile route. Seven million people crowded the streets to watch the motorcade go by.

An Investigation

In May 1951, Douglas MacArthur went back to Washington, D.C., for a time. Despite the great public support he had enjoyed, MacArthur had some important critics. United States Senator Richard Russell of Georgia headed that list. Beginning on May 3, 1951, Russell served as chairman of a committee that would investigate MacArthur's dismissal and "the military situation in the Far East."[4]

MacArthur testified before the committee for three days. Later, representatives from the State Department and the Pentagon were also questioned. The investigation resulted in nothing. The committee members finally voted to send the records of its hearings to the full Senate. It did not publish a statement supporting or criticizing the White House for its handling of MacArthur's dismissal. Nor did the committee issue a complete statement about changes that should be made in the nation's Far East policy.[5]

For a year after his return to the United States, MacArthur tried to explain his fears that Communists would not be content with controlling just North Korea but would eventually try to take over all of Asia. He stated his fears in the many speeches he made all over the country.

A Run for the Presidency

A year after his return to the United States, Douglas MacArthur was still very popular. Even though he was seventy-two years old, Herbert Hoover and other Republican leaders hoped he would agree to run for president in 1952. He refused, but did agree to deliver the keynote address at the Republican National Convention in July.

MacArthur's former aide, Dwight D. Eisenhower, won the race for president in November 1952. Before he took office, Eisenhower had lunch with MacArthur. MacArthur brought along a memo in which he argued that, on inauguration day, Eisenhower should make a public statement demanding that Joseph Stalin order Communist troops to leave both Germany and Korea and allow both countries to unite. If Stalin refused, MacArthur wrote, Eisenhower should order the military to drop atomic bombs on North Korea and China. This was all that would come of MacArthur's radical peace plan. Later, he would receive a short thank-you note, but neither the White House nor the Pentagon would approach him again for advice.

Fading Away

After 1952, MacArthur served as chairman of the board for the Remington Rand Corporation, now called Unisys. The MacArthurs continued to live at the Waldorf Hotel in New York City. Douglas and Jean MacArthur had both hoped Arthur would someday enroll at West Point. Instead, he attended Columbia University, from which he graduated in 1961.

Also in 1961, Douglas MacArthur made a final visit to the Philippines. In 1962, the new American president, John Fitzgerald Kennedy, invited him to the White House. Supposedly, MacArthur remarked while there, "I should have lived here."[6] Kennedy's successor, Lyndon Baines Johnson, invited MacArthur for another visit. In 1963, MacArthur helped settle a dispute concerning which American athletes should participate in the 1964 Olympics. Arguments had broken out between two organizations concerning what should be considered amateur status.

MacArthur also made a final appearance at the military academy at West Point. This would be a very nostalgic visit for him. He had always been very proud of his performance there, first as a student and later as superintendent.

An Old Soldier

In 1964, MacArthur's book, *Reminiscences*, was published. In January 1964, he turned eighty-four. His health had begun to fail. He had lost weight and complained of pain and fatigue.

On March 1, President Johnson made arrangements for an air force plane to take MacArthur to the Walter Reed Medical Center in Washington, D.C. Doctors feared he had cancer but found none during exploratory surgery. He did, however, have a weak liver and gallstones. He had surgery, but remained in critical condition. On April 3, MacArthur slipped into a coma. He died on Sunday, April 5, 1964.

When he received news of MacArthur's death, President Johnson ordered salutes to be fired in MacArthur's honor on American military bases all over the world. American flags were lowered to half-mast for six days, until MacArthur was buried. The nation was in mourning.

MacArthur's open coffin first went on display at an armory in Manhattan. On Monday, April 6, there was a ceremony in his honor at West Point. On Wednesday, April 8, his coffin was carried through the streets of New York in a funeral procession. The coffin was then loaded onto a funeral train, which took it to Norfolk, Virginia. United States Attorney General Robert Kennedy rode the train as an official mourner. Finally, MacArthur was buried in Norfolk. The courthouse was then dedicated as the MacArthur Memorial.

The MacArthur Legacy

In his own day, MacArthur was a very popular man. Army and government officials often found him headstrong, proud, and difficult to work with. However,

MacArthur's proud and defiant nature made him a heroic figure to many Americans, but offended many others.

the American public respected him for his many wartime victories. Today, historians look back at his role in the Korean War, seeing that he was right to fear the spread of communism, but they generally agree that he overstepped his bounds when he disobeyed direct orders from the president. He was a man whose pride and weaknesses were as strong as his brilliance and bravery. Despite the mistakes he made, however, MacArthur seems destined to remain one of the United States' most important military figures.

CHRONOLOGY

1880—*January 26*: Born in Little Rock, Arkansas.

1893—Enrolls in the West Texas Military Academy.

1899—Attends West Point.
–1903

1903—Commissioned second lieutenant in the army and
–1904   serves in the Philippines.

1904—*October*: Transfers to San Francisco.

1905—*October*: Receives appointment as aide-de-camp
         and tours Asia.

1906—Returns to engineering school, and also acts as aide
         to President Theodore Roosevelt.

1907—Gets transferred to Milwaukee.

1908—Posted to Fort Leavenworth, Kansas.
–1912

1913—Appointed to the army general staff.

1914—Goes on a secret mission to Mexico.

1916—Becomes assistant to the secretary of war.

1917—*October 18*: Sails with the Rainbow Division for
         Europe.

1918—*December 1*: Enters conquered Germany as
         commander of 84th Brigade.

1919—*April 25*: Arrives home a famous general.

1919—Becomes superintendent of West Point.
–1922

1922—*February 14*: Marries Louise Brookes.
         June: Accepts new assignment to the Philippines.

1925—*January 17*: Receives a promotion to two-star
         general, becoming the youngest in the army.

1925 —Returns to the United States to command III
–1927 Corps.

1928 —Returns to the Philippines.

1929 —Divorces Louise.

1930 —*November*: Becomes Army Chief of Staff and a
four-star general.

1935 —Returns to the Philippines to command its army.
–1941

1937 —Marries Jean Marie Faircloth.

1938 —Son, Arthur MacArthur IV, is born.

1941 —Recalled to active duty as Far East commander;
After the attack on Pearl Harbor, his troops retreat
to Bataan.

1942 —*March*: MacArthur, his family, and his aides flee
Corregidor; MacArthur commands Pacific forces
from Australia.

1944 —*October*: Invades the Philippines.

1945 —*September 2*: Japanese surrender to MacArthur on
the battleship *Missouri*.

1945 —Serves as ruler of occupied Japan.
–1950

1950 —When Communist North Korea invades South
Korea, MacArthur is designated commander of the
United Nations command in the Far East and fights
the Korean War.

1951 —*April*: President Harry Truman fires MacArthur.

1964 —*April 5*: Dies in Washington, D.C.

CHAPTER NOTES

Chapter 1. "I Shall Return"

1. William Manchester, *American Caesar: Douglas MacArthur, 1880–1964* (Boston: Little, Brown and Company, 1978), p. 271.

2. Douglas MacArthur, *Reminiscences: General of the Army* (New York: McGraw-Hill Book Company, 1964), p. 145.

3. I. C. Dear and M. R. Foot, eds., "Philippines Campaigns," *Oxford Companion to World War II* (Oxford, England: Oxford University Press, 1995), p. 883.

4. Vorin E. Whan, ed., *A Soldier Speaks: Public Papers and Speeches of General of the Army Douglas MacArthur* (New York: Praeger, 1965), p. 132.

Chapter 2. Childhood

1. D. Clayton James, *The Years of MacArthur* (Boston: Houghton Mifflin, 1970), vol. 1, p. 24.

2. Douglas MacArthur, *Reminiscences: General of the Army* (New York: McGraw-Hill Book Company, 1964), p. 3.

3. Ibid.

4. Ibid., pp. 4–5.

5. Sydney L. Mayer, *MacArthur* (New York: Ballantine Books, 1971), p. 12.

6. Ibid.

7. James, p. 16.

8. MacArthur, pp. 12–13.

9. Mayer, p. 15.

10. MacArthur, p. 5.

11. Lawrence S. Wittner, ed., *MacArthur* (Englewood Cliffs, N.J.: Prentice Hall, Inc., 1971), p. 3.

12. Quoted in Ibid., p. 5.

13. James, p. 27.

14. William Manchester, *American Caesar: Douglas MacArthur, 1880–1964* (Boston: Little, Brown and Company, 1978), p. 28.

15. "Fort Sam Houston," *The Handbook of Texas* (Austin: Texas State Historical Association, 1952), vol. 1, p. 632.

16. Manchester, p. 28.

17. Victor and Mildred G. Goertzel, *Cradles of Eminence* (Boston: Little, Brown, 1962), p. 92.

Chapter 3. Army

1. Lawrence S. Wittner, ed., *MacArthur* (Englewood Cliffs, N.J.: Prentice Hall, Inc., 1971), p. 4.

2. William Manchester, *American Caesar: Douglas MacArthur, 1880–1964* (Boston: Little, Brown and Company, 1978), p. 52.

3. Jules Archer, *Front-Line General Douglas MacArthur* (New York: Julian Messner, 1963), p. 28.

4. Manchester, p. 54.

5. Sydney L. Mayer, *MacArthur* (New York: Ballantine Books, 1971), p. 15.

6. D. Clayton James, *The Years of MacArthur* (Boston: Houghton Mifflin, 1970), vol. 1, p. 33.

7. Mayer, p. 15.

8. Ibid., p. 18.

9. Archer, p. 30.

10. Manchester, p. 69.

11. "Welcome to the US Army Corps of Engineers," *US Army Corps of Engineers Home Page*, February 11, 1999, <http://www.usace.army.mil/> (February 25, 1999).

12. James, p. 101.

13. Ibid.

14. Ibid., p. 107.

15. Wittner, pp. 3–4.

16. Editors of the Army Times, *The Banners and the Glory: The Story of General Douglas MacArthur* (New York: G. P. Putnam's Sons, 1965), p. 24.

Chapter 4. War!

1. Douglas MacArthur, *Reminiscences: General of the Army* (New York: McGraw-Hill Book Company, 1964), p. 45.

2. William Manchester, *American Caesar: Douglas MacArthur, 1880–1964* (Boston: Little, Brown and Company, 1978), p. 79.

3. Ibid.

4. Ibid., p. 84.

5. Ibid., p. 181.

6. D. Clayton James, *The Years of MacArthur* (Boston: Houghton Mifflin, 1970), vol. 1, p. 238.

7. MacArthur, p. 70.

Chapter 5. Back Home

1. D. Clayton James, *The Years of MacArthur* (Boston: Houghton Mifflin, 1970), vol. 1, p. 46.

2. William Manchester, *American Caesar: Douglas MacArthur, 1880–1964* (Boston: Little, Brown and Company, 1978), p. 113.

3. Sydney L. Mayer, *MacArthur* (New York: Ballantine Books, 1971), p. 33.

4. Ibid.

5. Dudley W. Knox, *A History of the United States Navy* (New York: n.p., 1948), p. 421.

6. Mayer, p. 34.

7. James, p. 157.

8. Douglas MacArthur, *Reminiscences: General of the Army* (New York: McGraw-Hill Book Company, 1964), p. 85.

9. Manchester, p. 140.

10. MacArthur, p. 83.

11. Mayer, p. 35.

12. Ibid.

13. William Gardner Bell, "Douglas MacArthur," *Commanding Generals and Chiefs of Staff, 1775–1995*, 1997, <http://www.army.mil/cmh-pg/books/cg&csa/cg-toc.htm> (February 28, 1999).

14. James, p. 365.

15. MacArthur, p. 99.

Chapter 6. World War I

1. Sydney L. Mayer, *MacArthur* (New York: Ballantine Books, 1971), p. 48.

2. William Manchester, *American Caesar: Douglas MacArthur, 1880–1964* (Boston: Little, Brown and Company, 1978), p. 162.

3. Ibid., p. 178.

4. William Gardner Bell, "Douglas MacArthur," *Commanding Generals and Chiefs of Staff 1775–1995*, 1997, <http://www.army.mil/cmh-pg/books/cg&csa/cg-toc.htm> (February 27, 1999).

5. Quoted in Theodore Friend, *Between Two Empires: The Ordeal of the Philippines* (New Haven: Yale University Press, 1965), p. 205.

6. Quoted in Manchester, p. 205.

7. Ibid.

8. Douglas MacArthur, *Reminiscences: General of the Army* (New York: McGraw-Hill Book Company, 1964), p. 117.

9. Manchester, p. 206.

10. Ibid., p. 194.

11. Ibid., p. 208.

12. John Devaney, *Douglas MacArthur: Something of a Hero* (New York: Putnam, 1979), p. 77.

Chapter 7. To Australia and Back

1. Jules Archer, *Front-Line General Douglas MacArthur* (New York: Julian Messner, 1963), p. 98.

2. William Manchester, *American Caesar: Douglas MacArthur, 1880–1964* (Boston: Little, Brown and Company, 1978), p. 232.

3. Archer, p. 100.

4. Manchester, p. 233.

5. Sydney L. Mayer, *MacArthur* (New York: Ballantine Books, 1971), p. 87.

6. Ibid., p. 88.

7. Manchester, p. 259.

8. Mayer, p. 89.

9. Archer, p. 107.

10. Mayer, p. 97.

11. Ibid., p. 99.

12. Archer, p. 128.

13. Ibid., p. 129.

14. Charles Messenger, *The Chronological Atlas of World War Two* (New York: MacMillan Publishing Company, 1989), p. 196.

15. Paul Boyer, et al., *The Enduring Vision* (Boston: D. C. Heath, 1993), vol. 2, p. 927.

16. Messenger, p. 239.

17. Ibid., p. 240.

18. Manchester, p. 466.

19. Quoted in Ibid.

20. Manchester, p. 464.

21. Mayer, p. 10.

22. Manchester, p. 499.

Chapter 8. Korea

1. William J. Sebald and Russell Brines, *With MacArthur in Japan: A Personal History of the Occupation* (New York: W. W. Norton, 1965), p. 92.

2. William Manchester, *American Caesar: Douglas MacArthur, 1880–1964* (Boston: Little, Brown and Company, 1978), p. 521.

3. Ibid., p. 524.

4. Douglas MacArthur, *Reminiscences: General of the Army* (New York: McGraw-Hill Book Company, 1964), p. 308.

5. Manchester, p. 507.

6. MacArthur, p. 313.

7. Manchester, p. 536.

8. "In the Cause of Peace," *Time*, July 10, 1950, p. 4.

9. Sebald and Brines, p. 184.

10. Ibid., p. 191.

11. Manchester, p. 554.

12. Ibid., p. 576.

13. Ibid., p. 580.

14. Ibid., p. 581.

Chapter 9. Along the 38th Parallel

1. Quoted in William Manchester, *American Caesar: Douglas MacArthur, 1880–1964* (Boston: Little, Brown and Company, 1978), p. 582.

2. Ibid., p. 584.

3. Ibid., p. 585.

4. Ibid., p. 586.

5. Philip B. Kunhardt, Jr., Philip B. Kunhardt III, and Peter W. Kunhardt, *The American President* (New York: Riverhead Books, 1999), p. 252.

6. William J. Sebald and Russell Brines, *With MacArthur in Japan: A Personal History of the Occupation* (New York: W. W. Norton, 1965), p. 217.

7. Manchester, p. 589.

8. Jules Archer, *Front-Line General: Douglas MacArthur* (New York: Julian Messner, 1963), p. 165.

9. Quoted in Manchester, pp. 590, 592.

10. Manchester, p. 595.

11. Ibid., p. 596.

12. Ibid.

13. Dean Acheson, *Present at the Creation: My Years at the State Department* (New York: W. W. Norton, 1969), p. 481.

14. Manchester, p. 620.

15. Quoted in Ibid., p. 624.

16. Manchester, p. 634.

17. Douglas MacArthur, *Reminiscences: General of the Army* (New York: McGraw-Hill Book Company, 1964), p. 395.

Chapter 10. Aftermath

1. Sydney L. Mayer, *MacArthur* (New York: Ballantine Books, 1971), p. 10.

2. William Manchester, *American Caesar: Douglas MacArthur, 1880–1964* (Boston: Little, Brown and Company, 1978), p. 655.

3. Vorin E. Whan, ed., *A Soldier Speaks: Public Papers and Speeches of General of the Army Douglas MacArthur* (New York: Praeger, 1965), pp. 251–252.

4. Quoted in Manchester, p. 664.

5. Manchester, p. 675.

6. Mayer, p. 9.

GLOSSARY

apoplexy—A stroke.

armament—Military equipment.

artillery—Large guns, such as cannons.

barrio—A ward, quarter, or part of town, especially in Spanish-speaking countries.

Confederacy—The Southern states that left the Union to form their own nation during the Civil War.

curvature—The state of being bent.

demotion—A decrease in prestige or position, especially in terms of military rank.

guerrilla—A soldier who fights irregularly with quick attacks or harasses the enemy and then retreats.

hazing—Rites of initiation, often including severe punishment, forced upon younger students by older students.

incompatibility—An inability to get along with another person.

intelligence—Information concerning the enemy, especially during war.

malaria—An often deadly disease that is transmitted by mosquitoes. Symptoms include chills and fever.

Mardi Gras—A holiday celebrated during the days leading up to the Christian religious season of Lent.

nationalist—One who supports or fights for the freedom and independence of his or her country.

neutrality—State of refusing to take sides, especially during a war.

peninsula—A piece of land surrounded on three sides by water.

FURTHER READING

Darby, Jean. *Douglas MacArthur*. Minneapolis: Lerner Publications Company, 1989.

Devaney, John. *Douglas MacArthur: Something of a Hero*. New York: Putnam, 1979.

Feinberg, Barbara S. *General Douglas MacArthur: An American Hero*. Danbury, Conn.: Franklin Watts, 1999.

Fox, Mary Virginia. *Douglas MacArthur*. San Diego, Calif.: Lucent Books, 1999.

MacArthur, Douglas. *Reminiscences: General of the Army*. New York: McGraw-Hill Book Company, 1964.

INTERNET ADDRESSES

The Avalon Project. "World War II: Documents." *The Avalon Project at the Yale Law School*. 1996–2000. <http://www.yale.edu/lawweb/avalon/wwii/wwii.htm> (August 25, 2000).

The MacArthur Memorial. n.d. <http://sites.communitylink .org/mac/> (August 25, 2000).

National Park Service. *Korean War Veterans Memorial*. July 30, 2000. <http://www.nps.gov/kwvm/home.htm> (August 25, 2000).

PBS Online. "MacArthur." *The American Experience*. 1999. <http://www.pbs.org/wgbh/amex/macarthur/> (August 25, 2000).

INDEX